Bursting Forth
with Fire

ISBN   978-1-716-28479-3

Self-published by Melanie Price (Through Lulu)

The author asserts the right to be identified as the author of this book

Acknowledgements
The sunflower image, included on the cover illustration, was derived from a photograph kindly made available on Flickr under Creative Commons (attribution licence)

Scriptures taken from King James Version of the Bible

Introduction

In writing this book I have been enthralled by the stories Melanie has related. It has been such a privilege to hear how she has been transformed by God's spirit touching her life. She heard God speak to her and responded with an eager heart to do His will.

My hope is that you will catch a glimpse of the sheer determination Melanie has to serve the Lord and how she has impacted people's lives along the way.

Melanie arrived one day with a huge shopping bag full of diaries recording the many trips and missions she has been on. "Where shall we start?" I asked.
"I don't know" Melanie replied, "at the beginning seems like a good place!"

Sue.

Musings....

I settle on the sofa near the window, relaxed and prepared to dictate the stories. As we begin to write the sun bursts forth and the sky is lit up. Under the sun there appears a golden halo beyond which there are white clouds edged with gold. They lead the eye of the beholder to a faraway land with trees in the distance, somewhere far, far away. From the halo a river flows, gleaming, sparkling and dazzling. Then after a moment it is gone. How quickly it all changes, just like life itself.

Melanie

Bursting forth with fire

There were many feet coming down the stone corridor and immediately a great fear came over me. I thought the worst, they've come to kill me, or even worse molest me or hold me for ransom. I'm dead!! It's my own fault Lord, I should never have come. All these thoughts swirled round my head. Dear Jesus, let it be quick, please don't let them touch me, or torture me.

By the time the men arrived at the door of my room I was hyperventilating…….they entered the room from the right and one man shouted,
"Butt, butt madame, butt."
I didn't know what it meant and by now I didn't care, all I knew was that I was one Christian woman in a locked building with these Muslim men and they had all come into my room. I shouted to them to get out but could hardly get my words out.

A word from the author

This book is a testimony of how God can take an individual from the pits of despair and a hopeless life and transform her into a useful vessel.

After being broken and remoulded by the Potter's hand I never intended to become an aid worker or a missionary, but God had other ideas. I have been going into the mission field now for over thirty years. When God spoke to me and told me to go, I could do no less than obey. Oh, what a life it has given me. I set off in 1989 and have not stopped since.

I started as an aid worker taking vital supplies out to Eastern Europe but as I grew into a believing follower of Christ, I saw an urgency for the gospel of truth to be told and to be proclaimed throughout the earth. Such a passion and fire grew in my soul to tell people about Jesus and what He has done for us that I cannot shut up, stop going or as now, writing about the wonderful way that God catapulted me into His work and I found myself not only Bursting Forth, but Bursting Forth with Fire.

I have been to many countries, evangelising, preaching, teaching, praying for people and nations, above all sharing God's love for them. Literally and spiritually, I took Jesus' command to,
"Go into all the world and preach the gospel to all creation."
(Matthew 28 v.19)
In doing so I have made many friends, discipled people and found a wonderful family of God where I finally fitted in, was loved and cared for. I hope you enjoy reading some of my adventures. It was difficult to choose, there have been so many and they haven't stopped yet.

The Sunflower Trust of which I am the founder and director is neither funded by man nor church but by God Himself in the most unusual ways. It is a giving charity with no overheads and in turn supports ministries in other countries.

6

Thank you

This book could not have been written without the script writer Sue, who is my dear friend and Christian sister. She listened and wrote for hour after hour and listened to all the bits in between that are not written in the book. She and her husband Ken devoted their time and efforts to perfect the book for the Glory of God. Without Ken's expertise in creating the cover, inserting the photos, his I.T skills and technology, bringing this book to fruition would not have been possible. God alone knows how many times the book caused them frustration, sleepless nights and hinderance but this sacrifice makes this book more priceless. Words can't give thanks and appreciation enough to this couple, but the success of this book will and their labour of love will not be in vain. God will reward them both with good health, long life and more blessings from God than they could ever dream of.

Love from M.

Contents

Contents

Contents

Contents

Bursting Forth
with Fire

by
Melanie Price

Chapter 1

Let me go, let me go, LET ME GO !!

I want to get out of here, I have had enough, I want to go. My children are grown up and I want to pursue the things that I have dreamed of, go to new places and meet new people and live a normal life, Let me go, let me go, LET ME GO! I have gone through enough. I have raised my children and I have been a faithful and hardworking wife. So, what happened to change the I, I, I, in me?

Well. I got saved, Yes, I ... BECAME ... A ... CHRISTIAN. God heard my desperate cry. He set me free from the chains that bound me to the travelling community, the violence, the alcoholism, motherhood and dissatisfaction with my life. I was at my wits end and yearned for something more. I longed for a peaceful life in a loving Christian community, maybe in Scotland where the air is clean, pure and fresh. However, God took me in a new direction which completely transformed my life.

By now I had become a cynic. My sisters-in-law had become "one of those Christians." I definitely wasn't going to be like them saying, "hallelujah and praise the Lord" all the time. Did they think I was a fool? I was not easily led and I certainly wasn't going to be led down the route they had gone. I didn't truly understand what to be Born Again meant. But there came a point where God and love won the day, when everything I thought I knew cracked like a piece of clay and I saw the empty and sad life I had been living. I hadn't really done anything about anything. I had just existed.

Something had changed in my sisters-in-law, something had softened in them. They started to talk about God, Jesus and the Holy Spirit of which I knew nothing, but I was envious that they had something that I didn't have. It was joy and a lightness, as though all their troubles had been taken away. They spoke differently, dressed differently, they didn't argue like they used to and they stopped rudely calling me "dinglar" or "divvy" and they stopped smoking! It was like a turn-around in their lives. Part of me wanted to be like them and be with them but the other side of me was thinking "I shall never be like that." Had they lost their heads this time?

There was a battle raging in me, "to be or not to be, that is the question." (Shakespeare). I mean they were, all five, good Catholic girls with a good, Irish, Catholic mother. But never mind, because as much as I loved her, she had lost it too!

Words to crack the clay

I eventually yielded when my sister-in-law Ruby told me that she loved me.
"You must be Born Again to go to heaven."
Then she went on to explain,
"I love you and you must give your life to Jesus to be Born Again. I love you but Jesus loves you more. I don't want you to go to hell."
These were powerful words. This statement flew from her mouth, it was the arrow that cracked the clay. Her words melted my heart.

The next Sunday I went to a little church in Darwen near Bolton and gave my life to Jesus. It was a very simple service with down to earth people. I found myself praying the prayer of repentance. But before the following Sunday came, something had stirred inside of me and my mind was troubled. I kept reflecting on the words of the prayer that I had repeated to the lady in the church, where I had to ask Jesus to forgive me for my sins. The word 'sin' stung.

I began to reason with myself. I mean I wasn't a sinner, I was a very nice person, I mean I worked hard at my fortune telling didn't I? I predicted good news about people's futures and I didn't even charge them too much for the service! I liked to help people as long as they were in the family, but outside of the family I didn't give a hoot. Yes, I was a nice person, well, a nice gypsy person, so what was the sin she spoke about?

I had to earn my living and I only stole little things so it didn't really make me a thief did it? I mean I wasn't a murderer was I, even though I thought about it many times. I thought I was a nice person but s i n, that word troubled me. I started to look up the meaning of the word sin. It wasn't in our everyday vocabulary. We would come out with a stream of foul and abusive language. Sin and salvation were new to me so I looked hard to see what sin really meant. The dictionary told me it was wrong-doing, unrighteousness, sinning against God, lying, cheating, stealing, evil thoughts, wicked deeds, jealousy, back-biting and swearing. I looked at this list aghast as I realized that I did all of these things.

I was beginning to become aware of my very sad state of life. I was really blind and wretched, deaf and devilish. My mind became even more troubled. As instructed, I started to read my bible beginning with the book of John in the New Testament. Then I read in Romans 4 vs.5,

"Jesus died on the cross to pay for my sins."
God cannot look upon sin. The "I" in me was troubled, very troubled.

The realization of my spiritual state was absolutely shocking to me. I had never even thought about these things before, I only related to God when I said, 'God bless you,' after I had told fortunes, not that God had anything to do with it, but that was my level of knowledge of Him. My life up to this point had been so intense, working day and night (in the summer) feeding the children, cleaning and trying to deal with my alcoholic husband's frequent mood swings. There was no room for God in my life or reason for having an extra burden put on me, i.e. God.

My husband John was becoming very dysfunctional and much preferred the company of the people in the pub to his wife and children which in many ways I can understand. John worked hard all day starting at six in the morning. It was very physical work, cutting trees, hedges and brambles, or collecting scrap metal. He was a conscientious worker and always did a good job. John had had a very serious accident in a head-on collision in the work van and was badly injured internally, resulting in three major operations. It took him over two years to recover, if he ever did recover properly, because when he was washed and dressed in his fine Irish tweed clothes, his leather brogues, his designer shirts with his well-manicured nails, you wouldn't think there was anything the matter with him. The scars from his operations were hidden from view and with a smile on his face he hid the mental and emotional damage he'd received.

He became full of fear and although he was driving again now, he was fearful of having another accident. He became overly fearful about everything, such as checking the door was locked at night, checking the gas turned off, pulling out electrical plugs. It seemed to him that everything was a potential death hazard. With his emotions so up and down we never knew what mood he would be in. This was not just attributed to the alcohol but to his mental state as well. I was beginning to learn about mental health and I really believed it was the accident and following operations that triggered it.

Something

Meanwhile at every given moment I was engrossed in my bible. I read the portion of scripture that says,
"God has not given you a spirit of fear, but of love, power and a sound mind." (2 Tim.1 v.7)
On reading and believing this, I could see that a spirit of fear was indeed a spirit, but not a spirit from God. I had actually thought this power from God was good health, I thought the love it mentioned was like the love I had for my children and a sound mind meant that I was not stupid (referring to my intellect). I certainly had lots of love and my mind was sound but on the

other hand here was my husband who was full of fear and whose mind was not sound.

The more I read my bible the more it spoke to me. It was alive, it comforted me and gave me understanding about opposing spirits. Well I thought I was already a very spiritual person, but it was not the spirit of God. Something was happening to me, my eyes were being opened, something was happening to my soul. I felt anxious about something. I was expectant that something was about to happen to me.

By this time, I had given my heart to the Lord. I had changed my job, continually read my bible, and I was being taught from the bible itself by visits to the Emmanuel church in Manchester. There were others on the campsite who were going through a similar process of becoming Christians, some denouncing Catholic beliefs, others giving up and repenting of fortune-telling, others learning from the bible and others dropping in to see just what was going on. But for me every word was a precious morsel of food for my soul.

Jesus became more and more a reality in my life and I was changing slowly, putting the old things behind me and searching for new things and new people, such as Christian people outside of my cultural environment. I found such loving, kind, genuine, God seeking folk out there who had overcome so many trials and problems because they had faith. Well, as you can see, I was speaking a new vocabulary, a new language, so even my conversation and speech had changed.

Bursting forth

Although all this was happening to me, I still had to provide for the family, try to cope with my husband and build on my new-found faith. I really was Born Again of my mind, my spirit, my soul and I was bursting forth with power. I became ignited every time I went to the church. I would be full of gusto and joy when I read the words of songs and praises on the overhead projector. Every song told the story of a father who wanted to pay the debt of sin for His children (me and you) by sending His one and only Son Jesus to take their place as a living sacrifice, so that they would be sinless, free, renewed, revived, uplifted and cleansed.

Oh, how many words are there to describe the wonderful metamorphosis that I was going through, like a caterpillar turning into a beautiful butterfly set free to soar. I cannot explain the wonderful feelings inside nor the tears I have cried for the depth of sin that had been in my life. I was so grateful that God had revealed His Fatherhood to me. I was not alone anymore. How could my husband deal with this, I was becoming a different person? I didn't want to go back to the pub, I didn't want to speak to his drinking buddies, I didn't want to swear, I didn't want to hear his meaningless, nonsensical conversation. This brought division between us.

However, he did become a Christian, yes, he did get baptised and yes, I believe he was sincere. I know that he loved Jesus but not to the extent that he would give up his drink or cigarettes for the Lord. Only God sees the heart of a man or woman and He knows the raging battle that goes on between the flesh and the spirit. The word of God says,

"For the flesh sets its desire against the spirit and the spirit against the flesh, for these are in opposition to one another so that you may not do the things that you please." (Gal.5 v.17).

This helped me to understand what was going on in John's life as the flesh was fighting against his spirit of good will to become a Christian. It was the same in me. I didn't have the Holy Spirit in me to fight the battle yet, but I knew about it. I had read about the disciples of Jesus who suffered the same things. Only when, after three years of being with Jesus and after He had died and risen into heaven, were they given the gift of the Holy Spirit. It came upon them in that upper room as tongues of fire and not just on the twelve disciples but on all who were present. It was interesting to me that the fire was in the shape of a tongue symbolising the spoken word of God.

Chapter 2

Orphans

I was no longer an orphan but adopted into God's family. The actual awakening of my spirit to see God's spirit had been happening between 1988 and 1989. I was Born Again in October 1988. I was married to John on 17th June 1989 in Emmanuel church, although culturally I had been his common law wife since 1967.

I was sitting in my caravan quietly and peacefully watching the T.V. which was positioned high up in the corner. A programme came on about the orphaned children in Romania. Shocking images were shown of archaic buildings housing hundreds of orphans. The footage showed little children with shaven heads who were sitting in rows of cots. They were rocking themselves backwards and forwards due to lack of stimulation and interaction with the staff and other children.

It was a true documentary and the presenter informed us that the current leader, Ceaucescu had implemented Decree 770 that all families must have five children. This was to raise the population levels in the country so that he would have greater numbers of people to go into the army and another generation of workers who he could tax and keep poor so that he could live in an opulent palace with an extravagant lifestyle whilst his people starved.

The native Romanian women were not allowed contraceptives, it became illegal to use them and of course being a Catholic country could justify it. The Romanian women were giving birth to babies that they could not feed so hundreds of thousands of babies and toddlers were placed into orphanages to be looked after by the state. This allowed the government to be rearing boys and girls for his army. Again, he could justify ownership of the children because they had become the state's responsibility.

The Romanian women felt hurt and ashamed that they had to give up their children. They secretly put them into orphanages which were in out of the way places, because the cities were not open to anyone and were heavily guarded.

God bless the people who made this documentary because a big secret was exposed to the world. Like me, many people who were watching it were appalled that human beings could be treated like this. The more I looked at the children on the screen the more upset I became. One young girl looked just like my eldest daughter when she was young. The big, round, soulful eyes looked at us helplessly through the screen of our televisions and pierced our hearts.

I couldn't sleep that night for thinking about those poor little children. Something had stirred in me, to say it was compassion is an understatement. I had a burning desire to do something, but I didn't know what. Something had to be done. I now believe it was God who placed a seed of that passion of compassion in my heart for those children and to help them in some way.

What can we do?

For weeks, more and more images were portrayed on the television and they just got worse. As the weeks passed, we saw that there were people from Germany, the U.K. and other European countries responding by sending out containers and lorries full of food. I noticed that there were appeals in the local shops for food, clothes, toys and toiletries to be donated. It was financed by staff of Bury hospital. They were called Angels of Mercy mission.

I quickly found out who they were and when they were going as I wanted to go with them. They told me that they were taking two lorries and joining up with others from other hospitals who were embarking on similar aid projects. I had no experience of acquiring great amounts of food and clothes, or raising money but when I put it to the family that I wanted to go to feed the starving orphans in Romania, yes, you guessed, they thought I was crazy, but they responded by saying they would help. The more I told people that I was going to Romania to help feed the starving children, the more people responded, offering their help and support and the more I convinced myself that I was going.

Preparing for the first trip

The practicalities of driving 2,000 miles into the Eastern Block had not really registered. Thank God for my naivety because I only counted the journey by how many days it would take to get there. I didn't consider breakdowns, trouble on the border or hijacker encounters. All I knew was that I was going a) to Bury and b) to Cluj-napoca. It was a four to five days drive. We were having an articulated lorry with a volunteer driver, so no worries for the journey. Well that was the plan!

Rita and I would be passengers who would ensure that the aid would go where it was supposed to go. Simple, dead easy, I didn't see it as a challenge, just a great adventure! After seeing all those poor children and the conditions in the orphanage, I was going to do something about it no matter what it took. I was going to get that aid to them.

The pastors from the King's Church in Oxford Road Manchester, near the BBC studios, had said that we could use their lower floor for storage, and indeed the aid came in by the ton. Clothes, shoes, bedding, toiletries, and off the shelf medicines were coming in via family and friends in the travelling community. They were also donating money which I put in a separate bank account so that I could keep account of what had been raised and what expenses I needed. In all fairness one can never know exactly how much is needed when embarking on such a journey.

It wasn't like I could say I was "trusting in the Lord" at that time because I was a young believer. However, I believe He trusted in me, for He was the one who put the passion in me to go. It wasn't even as though I knew the word of God (bible), but I did know that Jesus had said,

"Go ye out into all the world and preach the gospel of Good News to all creation." (Mark 16 v.15 NIV) and

"feed the widows and orphans." (James 1 v.27 NIV)

This was my simple understanding and it had to be executed, no matter what. With hindsight, as I reflect on it, I believe that it is something God instils in you to achieve and accomplish the mission in hand. I am quite a logical person and most things seem to be logically based. For example, if I needed to go to the moon, I would have to find a rocket, so I would go to Cape Canaveral rocket base!

Please don't think I am giving myself any praise. I was already having bible study meetings and we were learning about prayer. We prayed about the forthcoming mission trip. We asked in our new-found faith for the money and aid to come in. I was astonished when our prayers were answered and it did come pouring in! Apart from all the money and clothes etc. donated by the travelling people, help came from some very unexpected sources.

Amazing provision

I really wanted to take some baby food out. Now because I was still buying and selling industrial containers and pallets on my rounds in Wigan, I was aware of a big Heinz factory nearby, so the most sensible thing to do was to go and ask if they would donate some baby food. I tried to get to see the manager, but I was told to put my requests in writing and telephone him. So that is exactly what I did. Every time I rang to speak to Michael his secretary told me he was busy. I thought at first that it was because they assumed that I was a rogue gypsy woman looking for something for nothing (wrong thinking on my part). They had no idea that I was from that community for I hadn't told them. My only clarification of credentials was from the pastors of the church who verified that I was collecting aid and that I was taking a thirty-ton lorry out in August. It would be part of a convoy going from Bury hospital where aid was being raised by the nurses who were referred to as the Bury Angels.

The Angels were now advertising in the Bury Times and putting appeals on the local T.V. for their mission "Bury Angels mission to the Romanian orphans," whereas I on the other hand, a woman living on a gypsy caravan site, next to a tip couldn't possibly appeal or promote what I was aiming to do. The Bible says,

"A good name is to be chosen rather than great riches."
(Proverbs 22 v.1)

On reading the Bible, Jesus was showing me that there are names that are good and names that bad. I was beginning to realize that my name "gypsy" was bad and the name "angel" was good. This was one of the first lessons I learned. The name of Jesus is not only good but authoritative and powerful. But my name was neither good, authoritative, nor powerful. Things of the Lord are not as the world views things. I was an absolute nobody in a community of thieves and liars and never to be trusted. Even the word gypsy itself immediately conjures up something bad and something to fear. For were not the gypsies and Jews the most hated people on earth?

My point is that Jesus takes the most unlikely people to fulfil His will. Was not Jesus a Jew? And He came from a very poor family. He was also persecuted from birth and became a refugee when He was just an infant. His name, nevertheless, is the most spoken name in all the world. They said of Him,
"Can anything good come out of Nazareth?" (John 1 v.46 NIV) and there I was thinking,
"Can anything good come out of Crompton Lodges caravan site in Farnworth?"
Well yes it could, for we were now Born Again new creations worshipping Jesus. You can see how my thinking and mentality

was changing by learning about God as I read my bible. My mind was becoming renewed.

Back to the story

I finally got hold of Michael three let downs and six weeks later. He invited me to go and see him at the factory in Wigan. I went on my own, in a borrowed car, because I didn't want him to see my van at that particular time. He gave me ten minutes of his time, five minutes where I was able to explain what I was doing, where I was going and why. Then five minutes for him to tell me that he had great admiration for what I was doing especially as I was a woman with no big organisation behind me. Michael was only a young man in his early thirties and with a big, beaming smile he said,

"Come in tomorrow at two o'clock."

I knew then that he was going to donate but he didn't say what. I didn't care because it would be food of sorts. As I shook his hand and thanked him for his time I tentatively asked,

"Michael, should I bring a small vehicle or a big one?"

"A big one!" He answered.

I left his office with a spring in my step, knowing that we were going to get something big.

I returned the next day as instructed, to find that he had donated two tons of baby food and one ton of soups, vegetables, beans and other canned foods. I was absolutely overwhelmed to say the least. I now know that my persistence had paid off but more importantly I also knew that God was with me, for this was really an impossible thing unless He was in it. I promptly thanked the supervisor and drove the van directly to the church in Oxford Road.

Pastor Goos Vedder was the mission's pastor for Kings Church and it was he who gave me the facility to store the aid on the ground floor of the church as they held their meetings on the first floor. When Pastor Goos Vedder saw the extent of the aid he was amazed to say the least, at how God had brought in this

provision. It was now becoming more of a reality as the aid and money continued to come in. The money was to cover expenses such as fuel or anything else required for the lorries. The Pastor asked me if I would take some boxes of Christian literature and bibles to certain underground churches in Romania. I said, without really knowing what was in the boxes,
"Yes, of course."
I was learning to trust God and
    "walk by faith and not by sight." (2 Cor.5 v.7)
I say this because I was going into the unknown. I did ask myself, where is Romania? In those days Romania, Hungary, Ukraine, Poland, East Germany, Czechoslovakia and Bulgaria were behind the Iron Curtain. Thanks to my ignorance I knew nothing about this, but it was the uprising of the Romanian peoples in December 1989, a violent civil unrest, that they broke free from communist rule. It was a bloody revolution that rose up and led to the execution of the communist leader Nicolas Ceaucescu and his wife. (BBC World news Romania profile timeline 2018).

Hope Hospital

Hope hospital in Salford also made donations, this time of medical equipment. Again I just walked through the entrance of the main hospital and asked if I could see an administrator or director. It just happened to be at that moment that there was one available though I cannot remember his name. He was accompanied by a very business-like woman carrying a clip board. As he spoke, she recorded our words. I quickly stated my case. I had no qualification or clarification to say who I was.

Now it just happened to be at that particular time that they were closing down a ward. It had been used for filming a hospital T.V. series which was just completed. All the equipment had to be disposed of and I had come to the right place at exactly the right moment. I was given everything in that ward that my eye could see. I think there were around twenty-two beds, five incubators, drip stands, lots of boxes of dressings and surgical equipment. There were so many things I can't recall everything. Once again I had to borrow the big van to collect it all and take it the few miles to Kings church. The administrator was more than happy that he had disposed of the equipment and I was very happy that once again God had provided the essential equipment which was much needed. Oh how I was to find out the extent to which it was needed later down the line when it was delivered to a so called hospital in Romania. So here I was, accumulating a great tonnage of aid.

Disaster

I was amazed how many groups of people from outside of the community had heard about this woman raising aid to be taken out to the orphanage in Romania. They rung me and asked me to come and collect clothes, toys, toiletries and so many other useful things, including furniture. At Kings church the warehouse was filling up. All the pastors were surprised at the amount that had accumulated and wondered how it would be transported, including their Christian literature to be secretly delivered to certain churches and pastors.

I had secured a local company in Farnworth to take the aid out. I was being charged a greatly reduced rate because it was for charity. We had a thirty-ton lorry that was coming up from the south and was due to arrive in Manchester the day before we were due to leave and embark on our journey. I say we because we were travelling in a convoy with the other aid lorries bound for Romania on the same quest.

Well, that was my plan. All was going well until the day came. That day, I had arranged for the pastors, church folk and my family to come and help to load up the empty lorry as soon as it arrived. It turned into a disaster to say the least! Everything that had been stored was now loaded out in the street next to the church. We were waiting for a call to say the lorry was on the way. What we actually received was a phone call to say that the lorry had broken down just outside London and was not road worthy for the task in hand. My first reaction was disbelief and then anger, then of failure. I sat down by the kerbside and cried.

Now all the aid had to be taken back into the church hall. I felt embarrassed that I had not only let the church down, but also all the people who had come to help. I learned a valuable lesson that day about how I reacted when my plans did not come to fruition the way I expected them to. I was surprised by my reaction, but God was teaching me that His ways are better than mine. Man may have His plans, but I discovered that God's plans are definitely better. After crying for a while with sheer disappointment, I prayed aloud,

"Lord help me, what do I do now?"

Would I have to start all over again and find another lorry at a reduced rate? I may be logically minded but again the Lord was showing and directing me by His spirit as to what HE wanted me to do. I was a very young Christian and had to be taught how to listen and how to trust in Jesus. Hadn't I given my life to Him? Therefore, my life was no longer my own and I needed disciplining, teaching and directing by God Himself, because there was nobody else. Oh, how right He was, even now thirty years on I still marvel at God's wisdom and direction for this mission. I was to find out that it was far better to take two smaller lorries to cross the terrain rather than one big articulated lorry.

I felt led to go to Bury Van Hire and yet again God's timing was perfect. The national manager was there and was able to give me two lorries at a very reduced price because it was a charitable cause. One was a ten-ton lorry, the other a Luton box van. This meant that I had to drive one and find a volunteer driver for the other.

BUT God was putting His plan into action.

Once again I reported back to the pastors at the church and arranged for the aid to be loaded onto the street. This time I was driving and along with me was co-navigator and friend Rita. Two of my friends, both called John, had volunteered to drive the second lorry.

Oh, what a feeling that day, of excitement, adventure and euphoria of going into the unknown. I was actually doing it myself, because by now we were two days behind the convoy which had already left. After the men from the church, my daughter and grandchildren had helped load up the lorry I was finally ready to set off. What a glorious August day!

Before I left the pastors gave me the names and addresses of the pastors to deliver the Christian literature and the tracts in Romanian language to. I didn't deem that so important at the time but now realize that it was just as important as the aid. Then they anointed and blessed us and my family bade us farewell and God speed. We were on the night run down to Dover to catch the ferry to Ostend. The journey down to Dover went smoothly and the crossing was comfortable.

Ready to go ....

Chapter 3

Let the adventure begin.

The crossing to Ostend from Dover was relatively easy. The two lorries were loaded to the hilt. It was such a privilege that I could take the aid out myself but it was also a great responsibility. The aid was vital to those who would receive it. The tons of clothes, bedding and the medical equipment were so important and I had lots of it, as well as tons of life saving food. This wasn't just an adventure to me, but it was "feeding the 5,000" so to speak. Besides hadn't God Himself ordained the whole thing? Father God had changed my life by revealing His Son Jesus to me.

It was August and the weather was warm and getting warmer. It was relaxing and at the same time exciting on the ferry. We didn't know what was ahead of us. It was the not knowing that generated our real excitement. God had given us a mandate to go and here we were on the way. We took the midnight ferry, planned to rest during the crossing and then to keep driving until we reached our destination in Romania. I was driven by the compassion that the Lord had given me towards the orphaned children who were living without any love and in homes that were destitute. I had only seen it on the television, but the sordid images were enough to bring a nation into action. Many people and organisations had been prompted to go out in convoys of lorries containing aid of all kinds. Big companies and charities provided funding and there were lots of individuals who just loaded up their vans and cars with whatever they had and set off on an aid adventure holiday, some with their children.

So here we were, two Johns sharing the driving of the cargo lorry and Rita and myself driving the Luton van. Our plan was easy. I had mapped the route out on one piece of A4 paper. We were going to follow my pen markings. All I had done was to draw a straight line set at an angle from Bury, Manchester to Romania. It couldn't be easier! It was all quite clear in my head as I could simply see every country and city I needed to go through to reach our destination, all on one sheet of paper. Simple,......right??

Ostend in Belgium, Germany, Austria, Hungary and Romania, it was all very clear and as long as I had that map I could see where to go. My co-drivers were even more naïve than me.

Travelling companions

John Young (John Y) I had known since I was first with my husband John. He became a trusted friend. We were kind of neighbours on the same gypsy camps or stopping places. These were usually areas of waste ground in the North West area, as gypsies we were excluded from the rest of the society and living on tips and muddy, hidden places.

At that time, the government had started to make council sites for the gypsies. As the national population was growing the councils claimed all the common land for house building projects. Consequently, there was little room for gypsies or travellers. Some went to live on holiday caravan camp sites, but they were soon thrown off when they arrived with work vehicles, dogs and unschooled kids.

The other John, John Cunliffe, I had only known for a short time. I shall refer to him as John C. We met when my husband John needed a taxi to come home from the pub. John C, the taxi driver, was a Christian so John invited him into the caravan to meet me, his Christian wife! John C said his wife was a Christian too. My John invited him to stay for tea. He shared about his faith. From then on, he became a long-term friend and co-worker for the Sunflower Trust as the webmaster.

My husband John was like a time clock. He would get up at six in the morning for work, looking for scrap metal and weighing it in, or cutting trees etc. He came back at about seven in the evening, washed and changed, usually into a suit, shirt and tie. Then it was off to the pub, either on the bus or getting a lift from a family member or neighbour. Now this habit was formed because in English/Irish gypsy culture men and some women would go to the pub after a days' work. It became common that just the men would go, as there were often fights when the men got drunk. The men would congregate together, as they still do, to do business. Transactions were sealed with the slapping of each other's hands. It usually involved the buying and selling of horses, vehicles, or caravans. It was a great atmosphere. There would be singing of old Irish songs and even step-dancing in the older days. These little public houses did a roaring business with the travellers.

My husband loved the atmosphere. He could sing, tell jokes and dance. He was always the best dressed and usually the best-looking man. He wasn't fat or beer-bellied but was lean and of athletic build, he was also a champion boxer. Now this lifestyle may sound good but my husband, like many a good man, was taken into alcoholism which always brings a man to ruin. His personality changed completely, from being a hard-working family man to a violent, abusive alcoholic. His routine then became work, home at midday, off to the pub, back home around four just in time for tea. After eating his food (always meat) which I had earned the money to buy, he would go to sleep until seven thirty when he would return to the pub.

This life-style encroached on all the family and we all felt the changing moods of the man of the house (caravan). I did ask John if he would come with me to Romania but he said he was afraid and emphatically said,
"NO."
He thought it was a war zone as I had told him I was going into Arad, Romania, but through sheer ignorance he and the rest of the family thought I was going to Iran where there was a war.
John was trying hard to be a Christian but he didn't have the same passion as me. He had started to come to church on occasions, but at the first sign of problems, it was back to the

pub. I didn't blame him for not coming on the trip, after all he had three sons and they needed a wage. He was good at employing and teaching them how to work hard and earn a wage, but he was a hard task master and worked them like slaves. It was hard, physical work but the boys were kept busy and after all they were free for the rest of the day after an early start and finish. They didn't want to be with him for the rest of the day! They could see their friends on other sites and pursue their hobbies.

I was simply driven by my passion from Christ. I was a new Christian and God had given me a new chance at life. I was going just like the disciples went. I was going for my God and no matter what ever happened it didn't matter. Even if I died en-route it would be for my God and my country.

Rita

Rita my navigator, was little Rita Varey. I had only known her for a few years and she had become a very dear friend. She was a tiny woman, divorced and with four daughters still at home. Poor Rita had been through hell and high water. She had moved onto the caravan site in Bolton from Partington near Manchester because there had been some problems with the neighbours. She had someone to tow her caravan to the site where they gave her a plot in the far corner. She went out hawking, selling lucky charms and fortune telling every day. Some weekends she would go away to seaside places, staying in hotels where she would be the gypsy clairvoyant, giving palm readings and crystal ball readings. Various hotels would put on psychic weekends which would include spiritualists, fortune telling and clairvoyance. All this was quite legitimate for Rita and at least she was in the warm, whereas during the week she would walk door to door in all weathers.

The day after she moved onto the site, I went over to say hello and to meet her four daughters. They were beautiful girls aged between eleven and nineteen. The youngest was called

34

Little Rita even though she towered inches over her mother, as did two of the other girls, Bonnie and Michelle. The oldest one, Yvonne, was small in stature like her mother. I loved them from the moment I met them. I duly invited Rita to come over to my caravan to have coffee. In those days I had two caravans, one acted as a lounge come bedroom, the other was the kitchen trailer come children's bedroom. So Rita joined me in the kitchen the following afternoon about two o'clock and stayed until two in the morning of the next day. My husband had come home from work, been out and he and the children had gone to bed! I didn't want Rita to go. She was telling me things that were so catastrophic and heart breaking that it put my life into perspective and it humbled me.

I think one of the worst things she told me was about was when she was burned alive from a paraffin heater and as a result her limbs were fused together by the burning flesh. Even now, talking about it grieves me and brings tears to my eyes. This dear little soul spent two years in hospital. Any place on her body that was not burned was used for skin grafts on her neck. It's a miracle how she survived. We know that now, and through it all, the Lord was with her even though she didn't recognise it at the time.

I wasn't a Christian when I first meet Rita but I had already made my mind up that I was going to be her friend forever and that until the day she died or I died, I would be a sister to her. It was just like when I met my sister Rose, after eighteen years. I decided that I would never let her out of my sight again. I know these were Godly decisions even though I was not a believer at that time. God knew me long before I knew Him. I suppose I identified a lot with Rita because she had also had a husband who was an alcoholic. This meeting with Rita was about three or four years before I became a Christian in October 1988. Rita became a Christian the following year after a dramatic conversion.

Let down

So Rita became my best friend in the world and our children love each other to this day. On the day I married my husband (17.6.89) she let me down. John had become a Christian and we wanted to get baptised. However, because we were common law man and wife, we were told by the pastors that first we had to get married in church, in the eyes of God. Most people were shocked to discover that John and I weren't legally married and that we had five children and three grandchildren. Now with Rita being my best friend I wanted her to be my matron of honour. I was very nervous and anxious about the whole thing but I knew I had to go through with it. I was relying on my best friend for support. I wanted her there, I needed her there. She had become my sister and we were very close. We called each other "my Rite" and "my Mela." On the days leading up to the wedding I was so engrossed in the preparations, clothes, food, transport etc. that I took it for granted that Rita would be there with her four lovely daughters.

BUT, Rita didn't show up. What I didn't know was that my friend Rita had gone down south to do some fortune telling at a psychic fair in a hotel, she needed the money. I was really disappointed and upset with her. On such a special day,

HOW COULD SHE LET ME DOWN !!!!

I was so angry with her. It wasn't until a few days after the wedding that she gingerly came over to my caravan. I mean I wasn't going to speak to her, how could she be my friend and go somewhere else? When Rita came in, I was very cold towards her until with her opening sentence she sounded so distressed,

"Oh my Mela, I'm so sorry that I didn't come to your wedding, please let me explain."

She went on to tell me that she had no money whatsoever and out of the blue came an invitation to go to a psychic fair at a grand hotel as they needed a fortune teller/clairvoyant. She said that she desperately needed the money. By now my heart was already mellowing. I could never stay angry with Rita for long. I knew she had to be mother and father to her daughters and she had to put food on the table every day as well as provide gas and electricity. She had no other source of income except what she earned from the fortune telling. She excitedly went on to tell me that she had had the most bizarre experience in the hotel.

It stopped at the feet of a young man...

The story continued. She had travelled down with Laurel and Sophie who were also fortune tellers going to the same venue. All she had to pay was £10 for the table and £12 for her share of the accommodation. She borrowed the money and would have to earn that money first before she showed a profit of any kind. She said she had set her table display up with great pride because she had a five feet long star spangled and brightly coloured banner, which declared that she was a clairvoyant to the stars, film stars that is. There were photographs of famous people on it and one of her reading her crystal ball to someone. She had carefully laid her cloth on the table and placed the crystal ball in the centre. It was housed in a claw which was on a five-legged stand. It was quite large and took pride of place. She set out tarot cards and charms. Everything was set for business.

The doors opened at one o'clock and a stream of people came pouring in. Her table was strategically placed facing the entrance so that it was the first table people would see. A lady came to her table having first browsed the others which were in a semi-circle layout. She asked how much it would cost for a crystal ball reading.

"Ten pounds m'lady," Rita replied.

The woman pulled out her money and placed it on the table. Then the most extraordinary thing happened. The claw holding the crystal ball cracked and the crystal ball fell onto the floor. It rolled four or five metres along the room, down three steps and landed outside the door of the hotel. Rita said she ran after it for her life and she was very surprised where it stopped. It had stopped and smashed at the feet of a young man who was holding a banner saying,

JESUS IS LORD

On seeing Rita, his companions started singing and some were shouting that fortune telling was witchcraft and that it was an abomination to God. Rita enquired of him,

"What are all these ructions about?"

He replied,

"We don't want this witchcraft in our area because it is against God. No fortune tellers or spiritualists will go to heaven."

He told Rita to "Repent."

Rita told him she was a Christian but his response really shocked her,

"No you're not or else you wouldn't be doing this fortune telling."

Rita said she was speechless when he said that and she lowered her head and walked back to her table with the smashed crystal ball. Not knowing what she was going to do, she packed up her things and asked Sophie to lend her some money so that she could return home. Rita never, ever told fortunes again. Although she was penniless and very poor she knew that God had spoken to her and this was a sign that she must give up fortune telling. God Himself was moving in her life, teaching her and showing her His way.

When I heard this story, or should I say testimony I hugged her and cried. I loved her all the more for that. I knew that the God who was working in my life was working in hers too. Rita only had one brother and one sister who she hardly saw. They had idyllic marriages, families and businesses. Rita was a bit of an outcast, divorced, poor and now deserted by a lot of people in the community. BUT our God is a Father to the fatherless and a husband to the widow and deserted wives.

Rita went on to obey the Lord and came out on many missions with me around the world.

So when I asked "my Rite" if she would like to come with me to Romania, she did not hesitate. She immediately said, "Yes, my Mela, where you go, I will go."
There were so many capable and experienced people I had asked to come but they said no. God chooses His labourers so they can be blessed.

John C, John Y and Rita. A cup of tea and a song of praise

Austrian border guards

Chapter 4

Into Germany and Austria

After travelling through Belgium on the autobahn for a whole day we entered Germany. We drove into a pull-in so that we could sleep in the vehicles because we were very tired. How I remember that day, we had a problem with the border guards! I had parked in the waiting area so that I could show my documents to them, i.e. passports, insurance, vehicle logbook, credentials from the church and an inventory of the contents of the two lorries. However, it seemed that the border guard I was assigned to was having a bad day. I thought he had a Nazi spirit and he looked at me through cold, steel eyes. After looking at my documents, seeing that I was a Christian aid worker and a woman, he shouted at me and told me to go back claiming my documents were incorrect. I was shocked and quite taken aback to say the least and I went back to tell the team what had happened, but by this time I had already made my mind up that I would go further south to find another border crossing. That was the 'me' in me trying to work it out in the flesh and of course, my defiant spirit!

John Cunliffe deemed that we should pray, and that should have been my first course of action. The two Johns, my Rite and I set off praying and then a thought came into my head which I believe was from the spirit of God. I should take the lorries VIN plates, which show all the vehicle's details, and are fixed to the lorry near the steps. I promptly removed them and went back into the office to the same border guard and slammed them down (Nazi-style) and said very loudly,
"There!"
He didn't even look at them but just gave me a stamp of authorization to go into Germany. I came out laughing and with

a great feeling of victory. I learned a great lesson that day that we must not rely on our own efforts.

"Be careful for nothing but in everything by prayer and supplication let your requests be known to God." (KJV Phil 4 v6)

We continued on, driving through Germany without stopping until we reached Austria. This time the border crossing was a lot easier and the Austrian border guards were more welcoming. I can't continue the story without saying how beautiful I found the country of Germany. The diversity of landscapes from the flat agricultural fields to the beautiful mountainous regions, the descending valleys with their picturesque towns and quaint villages, especially Wurzburg. The amazing, forested areas and the meandering streams and rivers made a wonderful visual impact on me.

Arriving in Austria brought me into a new and challenging level of driving skills. We had to drive up and down mountains, not like the 'molehills' I was used to at home! The lorries were heavily loaded and I could only go at 40mph or in some places 20mph in second gear. It was the month of August the weather was glorious and it seemed to get hotter by the day. We would sometimes stop at a viewpoint and I would pull out my one ring gas camping stove, slice and fry a few potatoes, then add a tin of beans. We would devour them with relish accompanied by a loaf of bread bought locally en-route. The four of us would look out over the mountains which were still snow-capped even at that time of year. We would appreciate the artistry and creativity of natural beauty. The bible says,

"God saw all He had made and behold, it was very good." (Gen.1 v 31).

John C would get out his guitar and just there at the side of the road, we would sing our thanks and praise to the Lord our God who had given us the privilege of making that journey.

The route, through Europe was on the E80 autobahn which starts in Ireland and heads east passing through France, Belgium, Germany, Austria, Hungary, Romania and ending at the

Black Sea. It was probably built decades ago as a trade route between east and west and it is easily navigated. In Europe it is an easy road to drive on. It has been upgraded lately and may now even be called by other numbers.

Interestingly, I noticed that Vienna was spelled Wein on the sign boards. Then me being ignorant and naïve had also noticed what I thought was a well signposted town called Ausfart. On several occasions I would drive off looking for this 'town' where we could buy cheese, bread and fruit. Sadly, it was a 'rabbit trail' leading nowhere. I finally found out what it meant, 'EXIT!!' I felt enlightened. It became a source of much laughter.

Hungary

On the Thursday we had finally driven through Austria and arrived in Hungary on its western border, it was late at night and we were all very tired. We pulled into a place with a transport café and rested for the night. At 5.00 the next morning we refuelled and set off to travel through Hungary, passing through Gyor and Tatabanya. I was amazed how different it was to Austria. The land was flat and the roads were not as well maintained. I followed through on the E80 but I made a great error. The road divided into three junctions and I took the right-hand junction which led me off the E80 and brought me onto the outskirts of the city of Budapest. I felt a little anxious that I had taken this turning, but I knew that I was still on track even if it was the wrong one!

Budapest is the capital of Hungary. I knew I had to cross over the great river Danube as I headed east out of the city towards Romania. It would be signposted E80RO. You see Rita was my navigator, we had no mobile phones, or SAT NAV but we did have our A4 piece of paper with a map on and the line drawn from Manchester to Arad in Romania! As I entered the city I wound down the windows and the smells of the city flooded into the cab, rich aromas of coffee, pungent smells of garlic and all manner of food cooking as I passed the restaurants. I was enthralled and excited as I drove alongside the Danube, this wide, rapid flowing river had many diverse styles of bridges crossing over it from west to east. In fact the city was two cities, Buda on the west of the Danube, the hilly and mountainous side and Pest on the east bank is the flat side with wonderful open plazas and monumental squares.

Oh, what my eyes feasted on looking up at the Royal Palace, at the castle and St. James Basilica. I saw Gellert Hill, at the top of which is a Statue of Liberty. It is a girl holding a massive palm leaf in her hand to represent peace and liberty. It commemorates the liberation in 1947 of Budapest and Hungary from the Nazi rule and at one time it was to celebrate being part of the Soviet rule. Never-the-less the Hungarians loved it and did not want to take it down even in 1989 when they were liberated and became a democratic country. (att.topbudapest.org)

I was able to take in the most wonderful sights, including the iconic and magnificent Parliament building which is an exact replica of the Houses of Parliament in London. Of course, I didn't know anything about Budapest at that time, I just saw a breath-taking, fairy-tale city which I have never seen the equal of since.

Contrasts

We drove all day through Hungary. The quality of the roads had changed and they were becoming sandy dirt tracks. I was on N4 road heading east to Romania. Passing through tiny villages, I will never regret making that mistake of the wrong turning as I believe God was showing me that He would give me this nation for my inheritance. I was fascinated as I drove along these rough roads because there was so much to see. People were selling wicker baskets, hundreds of them, in all shapes and sizes. They were painted in pale pink, blue, and white and displayed on wooden poles. Others were selling terracotta pots and urns at the side of the road, some were selling enormous melons which were piled up like huge pyramids. We stopped to buy one and it was so heavy I couldn't lift it. We paid the equivalent of thirty pence for it! This turned out to be an excellent purchase as the weather was so hot, we used it as a cool, refreshing drink. It pleased my eye to see that horses and carts were being used for all manner of industry and business. Beautiful Hungarian palomino horses pulled carts loaded with sticks and wood. I saw a man pushing a bike with a big pig in a net tied at the back of the horizontal saddle. It was still alive! How he balanced it I will never know. The poor pig was probably off to market to be sold. People were selling chickens and in fact there was activity everywhere you looked.

The closer we drove towards Romania, the more evident the poverty became in village after village. We would see sewer dykes on each side of the road. The little houses would have water pipes extending from the roofs so that the water would run off and into the sewers. Now the smells had changed, I could smell wood burning as each little house had smoke billowing out of their chimneys.

Everything changed and unfolded to reveal a different Hungary. It was now a far cry from the beautiful city with its ornate palaces and architecture. Now I could see the reason for coming. My heart was excited and anxious at the same time about what I was going to see further down the line. As the evening came on, later as it does in August, we welcomed the coolness of the air. Remember that we had been up since five that morning and we had driven with a stop here and there to make something to eat, such as beans, fried potatoes, soup, bread, apples and melons. I had always understood that we were going to feed the poor so how could we expect anyone to feed us? I had packed some provisions for the four of us for two weeks. I don't remember that I had any of the currencies of the countries that we were passing through and in those days there was no E.U. I bartered soaps, shampoos, chocolate even cigarettes for fresh bread, fruit and eggs as we went along the way.

An uneasy feeling

By now it was getting dark and I had to drive up a very big hill. I was tired and so was John Young in the other lorry but we had to make headway. Having driven across Hungary in one day, I decided we would pull in at the first opportunity that I could see, even in the dark. I hadn't consulted the Lord on this plan because as yet I just saw myself primarily as an aid worker, then as a young believer who still only knew how to do things herself. So, as ever, being that logically minded young woman, all I knew was that we needed sleep and something to eat before we entered Romania the next morning in daylight.

The night seemed very dark and there were no lights on the road but up ahead I could see the lights of a building. As we approached I could see that it was a panzio, the equivalent of a bed and breakfast. It had a big car-park so we pulled into it with the two lorries. I was so glad to step down into the cool of the evening and stretch out my arms and legs. I sent John Y into the building which was dark and gloomy apart from the one light. There were three men sitting at a table and they were drinking what looked like vodka. The men, seeing John as a stranger, invited him to sit down and offered him a drink. I knew that John was not a drinking man and not the best at communicating so he couldn't tell these men what he wanted.

After a while when he hadn't come out, I decided to go in to see what had happened to him. I was always very aloof, alert, suspicious and mistrusting of everyone in those days. My plan was that we two ladies would sleep in a bed for the night and the men would sleep one in each lorry to guard them. I walked in boldly. The men were astounded to see what they thought was a Hungarian woman looking for a room so late at night. I put my two hands together and alongside my face to gesture that I wanted to sleep. Hopefully they would understand that I was looking for a bed. I had an uneasy feeling when one of the men took me up a narrow staircase to show me a tiny room with a small double bed in it. My mind quickly went into overdrive as my impure thoughts put fear into me. It was an easy equation, four men drinking, one foreign woman and a double bed. Fear traumatized me, and the realization that they may have thought I was a prostitute. If John got drunk or I was sleeping in the room upstairs and if the men knew the precious cargo we were carrying, it might have all disappeared by morning. All these thoughts bombarded me. Whether it was my fear or a check in my spirit I decided to act like a crazy woman. I spoke to John Y in Romany language,

"Kaker peev, jellakai." (Don't drink, let's go!)

Then I started hitting poor John, shouting at him very loudly as though I was his wife who didn't want him to be drinking. It shed a whole new light on the scene and changed the atmosphere. It worked. John ran out of the door as if he was really upset. I wanted us to leave as soon as possible. Tired as we were, we jumped into our lorries quickly and hit the road. I thanked God that I had had that check in my spirit and that I didn't stay in that little panzio and give in to my tiredness.

Forewarned

Then later, there was another incident that happened as we were climbing up those mountains. It was steep and the lorries were struggling and chugging along in second gear. It was still dark and the road almost a single track. I spotted the headlights of an oncoming car. The car slowed up a little as it went passed us. I saw that it was a black Mercedes but didn't take too much notice at first but then just a few minutes later I noticed in my mirror that a car was trailing behind us. Although it was behind the second lorry there was no reason why it couldn't overtake us. There were no other cars on the road at that time of night. After a few more minutes the car did overtake but as it passed by it slowed down and the driver, a man, looked into the cab of my lorry. Then he took off at high speed and disappeared into the darkness.

The next thing that happened was very frightening and I knew the driver of the car was scouting. Fear set in once again and I didn't dare tell Rita what was going through my mind. I thought they were hijackers. Thank God for my education in the world of travellers where I learned that men would go night scouting for lorries loaded with precious metals. They would deliberately stop the lorries and ask for help and then throw the driver out. One man would get in and drive the lorry off and the other would follow and before daylight the metals would be stored somewhere else and the hijacked lorry abandoned. I had already been warned of this by Gypsy Joe Smith's cousin and that on no occasion was I to stop if anyone tried to pull me up.

When I saw the headlights coming towards me for a second time, I realized that the car was on my side of the road. He flashed his lights at me to stop. Rita didn't know what was happening. I told her not to be afraid and not to say anything. I was forced to stop and of course John had to pull over too. I tried to be brave and vowed to myself that they were not going to take my load but when push came to shove I crumbled and fell nearly apart. I persuaded myself that first and foremost I had to preserve our four lives. Our lives were more precious than the cargo. I made my mind up that if they had knives or guns, I would surrender the lorries and their cargo without a fight.

Hmmm, what happened to my ethics of guard the aid with my life? Now being put to the test I failed miserably. As I saw the two men walking towards the lorry, I realized my only option was to pray.

"Pray Rita," I shouted out to her.

Then I prayed aloud,

"Jesus do not let the men hurt us or take the cargo."

They came to the passenger side where Rita was sitting and seemed a little taken aback to see two women. For a moment they stared in disbelief. I had been warned about the dangers of being hijacked by the Roma mafia. I gained eye contact with the man who was by now speaking to Rita. I couldn't understand a word. As I opened my mouth the Lord brought back to my mind the Romany language I had learned and I greeted them with,

"latcho rati." (good evening)

They seemed shocked to hear me speak the Romany language. I continued on gently and sweetly,

"ma pral soski?" (my brother, what do you want?)

Again shocked they replied,

"Shemmi." (nothing)

Before they could utter another word the Lord opened my mouth again and I said,

"tut kamav Jezus? (do you love Jesus?) Amensa gell Romania (we go Romania) O hobin e chaves. (we have food for the children) Roma chaves nixs daddus, nixs ama (children with no fathers or mothers)."

"Devla vorba gell Jezus nave, (God said go in Jesus name) Hobin e bitsi Roma baram." (feed my little Roma lambs)

Still in total shock and embarrassment he pointed to my therapeutic back rest made of wooden beads and balls and gestured that I give it to him. So we gladly gave the men both of the back rests without getting out of the lorry and then wished them,

"Te del O del." (God bless you)

After that they returned to their car and took off at great speed. Meanwhile John Young came to ask me what had happened. He explained that they didn't get out of their lorry because they thought it was the police and didn't want to be intrusive or complicate things. It was a good experience to reflect on as I knew that God had been with us. Once again I learned a lesson that I should not look to myself but,

"Trust in the Lord with all thine heart and lean not on your own understanding. In all your ways acknowledge Him and He shall direct thy paths." (Prov.3 v 5-6)

Finally, at a safe distance we pulled into a lay-by and slept for a few hours, me with my head on Rita's lap and her with her head on my shoulder.

Border Guards

As dawn broke we set off once again. Even though this was my first aid and mission trip I would never abort it or leave the aid in those two vehicles until it reached the people it was purposed for. Those lorries were loaded with life-saving equipment, medicines and food etc. To me, God had sent me, God would help me, God would guide me and God would protect me. No way was I leaving those lorries until I had delivered the contents. I thanked God that I had had that check in my spirit and that I didn't stay in that little panzio and give in to my tiredness.

We continued on until we reached the Romanian border at about five in the morning. It was a good thing that we arrived so early. Already the queue of big lorries must have been two kilometres long. I say this because it was to my advantage, as many of the lorry drivers were still sleeping in their cabs, so I very boldly drove past them all. The drivers who were out of their cabs were angry and raised their fists in protest, but I just put my foot down until I reached the border guard station. The two Johns followed boldly.

The guards looked astonished when I, a woman, climbed down from the cab. I looked at them and realized that they were very young men. They were all dressed in blue uniforms and wearing peaked caps. Each one held a Kalashnikov semi-automatic rifle which surprised me and gave me an uneasy feeling.

Romanian border guards

When I made eye contact with them I believe the Lord allowed them to see me as a mother figure and indeed, when I looked at them all I could see were five or six frightened young men. In that fear they would have used those rifles if they needed to.

On the lorry dashboard I had some soap and toothpaste which I used for bartering for eggs en-route, they looked at them and pointed. Now I knew the score and so did they, so I offered soap and toothpaste to each one and I even had some cigarettes to offer. Once they had received them they beckoned me into the inspection area. I kept smiling all the time while the inspectors came to check our passports and the inventory of the contents of the lorries. They tried to keep straight, serious faces to show their authority whereas I, having no authority, did the opposite and laughed and giggled, thanking them so that they would allow me to continue across the border without further hassle. The memory of the German-Austrian border was still fresh in my mind. As Melanie always has plans, a, b and c, I was already devising plans as to how I could get things done my way. However, I cannot take any credit or glory for when the barrier went up, he simply waved me through followed by the two Johns. I was ecstatically happy when I drove through smiling and waving. As I looked back I could see the other lorry drivers still hurling insults and gesticulating.

Romania at last!   Nevertheless, it was praises and hallelujahs to thank the Lord as we drove along the single tarmac road on our adventure.   Slowly moving on for an hour or so I noticed that the tarmac road had become more of a dirt track. The scenery outside had completely changed and it felt different. It was like we had stepped into a time warp, or into a medieval land.   I saw that the fields had been harvested of hay and it was gathered into sheaves.   They had stuck a stick into the ground then woven the hay round it to create a cone shape, with the remainder of the stick poking through the top.   I had not seen this type of haystack before.   In Hungary I had noticed that they create sheaves as they did in biblical times.

Romania

The early morning sun had risen and the heat of the day could be felt.   It was around nine in the morning and we decided to pull over and get something to eat, even more importantly we needed to breathe in the atmosphere of this new country which felt quite strange as we had never seen anything quite like it before.   Out came the camping gaz stove and the frying pan and into it went the eggs which we had bartered for in Hungary.   That first meal in Romania was delicious.   I can almost smell and taste it as I write.   The flat chips, eggs, beans and the remnants of the Hungarian bread were delicious as ever.   How we enjoyed our meal even though this was basically how we had eaten along the way. There was no stopping at cafes or lots of hotels for us. We couldn't justify the expense for four of us, and it is my nature to be self-sufficient. After having five children one knows how to live economically. This was my way of thinking before I became a Christian. Some may say it is out of a poverty mentality, but I see it as being sensible and conserving our resources. After all this was not a holiday.

God recompensed me well. He has taken me to dine with government ministers, to stroll through king's palaces, and to hear great operas in Austria and Hungary. I have surveyed castles and eaten the most wonderful cuisine with rich and poor but as for now, this being 1989 my ethos was that if I was going to feed the poor then I should not take anyone's food or use their resources. I still think the same thirty years on.

Feeling replenished from our meal we set off again to drive through towns and cities which were quite eerie. I remember looking at the scenery again. We encountered huge pipes as high as a house and others running horizontally, they were corroded with rust, evidence of industry that had long ceased to be. The eeriness came from the lack of people, just here and there we noticed an old lady dressed in black with a black scarf on her head. In the towns where I thought I might get bread I saw long, long queues of people outside the bakery and it seemed they were limited to one loaf, presumably at an extortionate price.

We didn't really have time to stop and queue. I knew how to make gypsy bread, cooked in three minutes in a frying pan. We stopped a few times along the way to eat from our little kitchen which comprised of a cardboard box containing a gaz stove, a frying pan and a few provisions. We knew how to live well!

Romania is a vast country and I knew we had to navigate through the Transylvanian Alps. As yet we were still on long flat roads. We came to a junction and I took the left turn to Cluj-napoca. It was getting late and now we were in Romania I thought that we deserved some more sleep. This was the fourth night of our travels. I pulled into what looked like an antique looking hotel situated at the foot of the south Carpathian Mountains known as the Transylvanian Alps. We slept in the lorries on the car park which was spooky and dark.

The next morning, we gathered our belongings and prepared to leave heading for Cluj-napoca. Why Cluj-napoca specifically? It was because the mission pastor, Pastor Goos Vedder, from Kings Church, Oxford Rd., Manchester, where I had stored the aid, had given me the names of the towns, cities and the people that I was to take the aid to.

Cardboard box kitchen. Making eggs, chips and gypsy bread

Chapter 5

Cluj-napoca

After driving on about sixty kilometres we arrived at our destination. I was horrified at the state of the place. Just seeing the people dressed in rags indicated to us that this was one of the worst hit cities. Here we saw people picking up every scrap of rubbish to make fires and were actually cooking in the street, maybe just a potato or a few vegetables. They were queuing for bread just as in other places. The peoples' faces were sombre and full of hopelessness and despair. They all turned their heads to look as they heard the sound of the diesel engines of the western vehicles. They must have been thinking that we had arrived with something for them, and we were thinking that we had better get out of that place before we got mobbed. Indeed some people did run towards the lorries, so we just kept on going. As the leader I had to make some tough decisions. The fact was that we weren't hungry as we had enough provisions and I had to stick to the agenda of what we would eat and when. We just needed some fresh bread about every two days.

We drove down to a quieter little area to ask for directions to John Pop's church and house. We asked one lady who was a road sweeper. Her face lit up with delight as she gestured, with her arm, the way we should go. She said her name was Coralina. She told me that she had to sweep the road to get a miniscule wage from the government with which she had to feed her five children. With great expectation she asked if we could help her. I asked her to write her name and address on a piece of paper and I assured her I would be back later in the day. My heart had connected with her. However, my priority was to deliver the bibles first and then the medical equipment to the hospital.

We eventually found John Pop. It's funny how certain names suggest a pre-conceived idea of what someone might look like. I thought he would be an old man as the name Pop suggested a father figure. In fact he was a young man, in his mid-thirties and dressed in a suit. He had a soft, gentle nature and had an incredulous look on his face when he saw a woman driving the lorry, but his astonished look soon became a big, beaming smile. He was a friend of Pastor Goos Vedder. He had been expecting a man to come discreetly in an unmarked vehicle to drop off the Romanian bibles. The bibles, about seventy-five of them were wrapped in five parcels with brown paper. They were discreetly carried into John Pop's house.

Next we followed him in his car for about thirty or forty minutes out of the town. In his broken English he told us that we were taking the beds and incubators to the hospital. One thing I do remember was that as we approached the place I could see a high wall and a gate. It looked more like a prison entrance. When we entered through that gate I will never forget what I saw.

Unforgettable

The courtyard was made of old cobble stones and we positioned our lorries together in the middle of it. The patients who were wandering about suddenly stopped, stood still and stared. In their amazement it was I, a woman, who disembarked.

Someone gave a shout of delight and the people came rushing towards the vehicles. There were lots of amputees. I remember they had few or no clothes on, some had small cotton sheets wrapped around them, marked with blood and excrement. One man had a yellow rubber glove stuck to his side used as a stoma bag. I could see scars on peoples' necks and bodies from recent operations as the roughly done stitches protruded like stitching on a moccasin shoe. I do not say this lightly for these were real people. The smell was nauseating, in fact it was urine, blood and excrement. It was terrible.

As they rushed towards us we were frightened and jumped back into the lorries and locked the doors and windows. Meanwhile John Pop and about five of the staff, who were dressed in a white coloured uniform, came running out and shooed them away with authority.

We were invited into the hospital building where very emaciated men, women and children looked on, some peeping round corners of the building. The hospital director had summoned all the male staff to come and help to unload the lorries. The two Johns and staff only took out what was listed on the inventory for them. Rita and I were escorted into the hospital building. I had already decided that I wanted to leave as soon as possible and get back to Carolina - that was my selfish ambition. The director wanted to show us round the hospital but I quickly said no as we had a time schedule. However, he took Rita and I along with John Pop round to the back of the building where there was a separate building, an extended shed really. I was aghast at what I saw.

Hospital kitchen

There were long, metal trough-type tables in the middle of the room which were filled with charcoal, or some sort of coal and wood. This was where they cooked. There were several huge cauldrons bubbling away, one was full of cabbage. The cooks were dressed in off-white uniforms and wore hats and white clog-like shoes. It was very hot in there and it amazed me how they were coping with the heat. It was around midday by then, it was so hot outside and I for one was sweating. I had seen enough. I had delivered my goods and now I just wanted to get out of this hell hole, a breeding ground for all kinds of bacteria and infections. Instead the director said we must stay for lunch. At that my mouth took over and was speaking the words, "OH NO, NO WAY!"

The shock must have been evident on my face but they insisted. So we found ourselves reluctantly seated at a plain wooden table covered with a table cloth, outside in the middle of the courtyard. One of the staff brought some white bowls and spoons. A steaming cauldron was placed on a chunk of wood on the table. The director bade us sit and enjoy the meal. We sat in anticipation waiting for some vegetable soup. We couldn't contain our shock when the ladle produced a grey liquid with one or two lumps of fat and what looked like rice balls floating in it. I thought in my self-centred way, I can't eat this. My mind was on overtime as I thought it may be a bowl of germs from unwashed hands. These thoughts were fuelled by the increasing stench of bodily fluids permeating the air in the heat of the day. I wanted to be sick but I knew I could not leave the table. My faith wasn't so strong in those days but I was very glad when Pastor John Pop prayed over the food. Those words had power and I lifted the spoon to my mouth to taste that grey substance. It was my first taste of Romanian soup. I knew that I had some "safe" dried cuppa soup in the lorry cab. I managed to eat a couple of spoonfuls, but I was sure it would not go to waste if I left it as it seemed a thousand eyes were watching us.

Back to Cluj

Oh my selfishness had risen, did I really care for these people? These thoughts ran through my head. Did I care? What about the little boy wearing a little shirt which barely covered his private parts, his little face writhed in pain? Or the old lady whose back was so badly bent that she could only look at her feet, which by the way, like the other patients, were bare. They had no shoes yet had to walk on the cobbles.

To speak more bluntly it was more like a concentration camp or medical camp of Dr.Mengele in the days of the Second World War. Dr.Mengele was a Nazi doctor who performed atrocious experiments on the Jews so that he could learn how to treat the German soldiers in the field hospitals. I know about this because one of my closest dearest friends Madam Hortense Daman Clews was a Great War hero who saved 180 allies during the war. The story is told in her book "A Child at War (Bles M. 1969). She was a young girl of seventeen from a place called Leuvan in Belgium. She would ride her bike through the streets with hand grenades and weapons in the front basket and covered with groceries and eggs. She was part of the underground, like the French Resistance. She was caught and sent to Ravensbruck, where she was injected with gangrene so that the effect of it on her body could be observed. She told me, privately and personally, what the hospital there was like and here was I in a hospital very similar to that.

As soon as we could we thanked them for our meal and quickly climbed into our lorries. All the people waved and smiled. Off we went hastily. We wanted to get back to Coralina in Cluj-napoca because it seemed a more normal thing to do and it was away from the stressful sights we had experienced. But first we followed John Pop to a village about ten miles outside Cluj. It was a quiet suburb within Cluj and we were taken to the local Pentecostal church where we were surprised to find three other pastors waiting to greet us. We weren't too sure what was going on, especially when we also noticed a large group of women and children, all with big smiles on their faces, waiting for us. We soon understood that they were waiting to help unload the food and clothes from the lorry. They sung beautiful Romanian Christian songs, like Amazing Grace, which we recognised from the tunes. The songs seemed much more spiritual when sung in Romanian.

Unloading provisions

After they had unloaded their share of the supplies, a man called Valentine invited us to go to his church to meet the Romanian gypsies. We were introduced to the waiting congregation and gave them gifts of toiletries, soap and clothes. They were so shy but happy that we had come and happy that we cared. After many waves and goodbyes we followed John Pop to that Transylvanian Hotel where he had booked us in free of charge as guests of the town.

Coralina

After John Pop had gone, we headed back to find the street where Coralina lived, a dirt track really. She didn't invite us in. No wonder, for at the sound of our lorry coming down the road the children, half dressed, tumbled out of the house. It was a sight I hadn't seen before. One child wore a pyjama jacket, another the pyjama bottoms, the others were scantily dressed in rags. The little hovel of a home was falling apart and a piece of corrugated iron served as a roof. My heart was full of compassion and emotion. The seed of love was beginning to germinate. All I could do was kiss and hug them, as did Rita and the two Johns.

Coralina and her family

John Y picked the little one up in his arms and cuddled him, he was about two years old. Coralina said she had a seventeen year old son but he couldn't come out as he had no trousers. At that I went into the back of the lorry and found some trousers and made a box of clothes for the other children. I knew it wouldn't solve the problem but would ease it for a few days. We gave them some food too. Coralina and her little family jumped up and down with delight, hardly believing that they had been given food and clothing free of charge. Eventually the seventeen year old came out, wearing the trousers which he had tied up with string to hold them up as he was so thin. All of our conversation was done with gestures, smiles and hugs because we didn't speak each other's language. Everything was done with love which doesn't need translating!

By now it was late and we were tired. We returned to the hotel. I still hadn't finished my mission, but for now we needed some sleep.

Transylvania Hotel

The hotel resembled something out of a horror movie. We parked up on the dirt car-park and I made my way to the huge, thick, wooden and studded door and entered boldly into the large reception area. It was of palatial size with a small reception desk. I rang the bell for attention. Out came a very slim man, dressed in trousers, shirt and black jacket. He spoke to me in Romanian. From an educated guess more than any knowledge, I deduced he was asking how many rooms I would like. The Romanian language base is Latin, a far cry from Slavic-Hungarian language, so I spoke in my best French!
"Deux chambres, s'il vous plait" (two rooms please)

To my amazement he understood and brought out a big book to see which rooms were vacant. He gestured that there were two rooms on the first floor. The whole building appeared to be three or four storeys high as in Baroque style. It had been magnificent in its heyday and I discovered later that it was once used by the recently assassinated Ceaucescu as his summer residence when it was known as The Belvedere. The man gave us two keys. By now I could smell the foisty soft furnishings, but I couldn't smell coffee or food which I thought was quite unusual. I told Rita and the Johns to leave their bags and go down for food because we were all hungry. We went down to the fine dining restaurant to find out that it was so fine that they had no food, not even a slice of bread! I was gutted to say the least. I gestured to the man to bring what he had. After about five minutes he arrived with four beautiful white china plates edged with gold and a raw cabbage leaf and a slice of capsicum. We were offered a glass of water.

Rita and I were so tired and hungry that we decided to go to the lorry and get a cuppa soup which satisfied our hunger pangs. The two men were not having that and decided to drive into the town and find some bread and real food. Tiredness had overtaken me so I didn't argue.

Rita and I decided to sit a while in the lounge. All of a sudden music started to play and it was English dance music. Rita being Rita was up and dancing on her own. Meanwhile a young and well-dressed man came over to me and asked if we were English.

"Yes." I replied, after all he was quite a handsome chap.

Rita beckoned me over to the dance floor, so I joined her leaving the man at the table. When he saw that we were enjoying ourselves he came over to dance with us. Very quickly Rita and I sat down, after all our culture doesn't allow us to dance with strange men. Oh, by the way, just to say that apart from our group and that man there was no one else in the hotel. The man told us his name was Daniel. It was refreshing to talk to someone in English other than my companions.

He started asking what we were doing in Romania. Rita and I were very keen to tell him that we were co-workers and we had come along with two men, with aid for the poor children. He thought it was admirable and had seen the two lorries parked up earlier. We went on to ask what he was doing in Romania as he had said he was a Hungarian businessman. He told us that he had come to Romania to buy antiques from the poor village people and then he would sell them in Germany at an extortionate price. At this I was aghast because I now realised that he was preying on the poor. Those poor people were selling their ornaments and antiques just to buy food at an equally extortionate price. I really didn't like him as he was the exact opposite of what I was about. He was taking from the poor and I was going to give to them.

Rita got up to go in search of the ladies room and I was left at the table with Daniel. He enquired,

"How much money are you getting paid for this trip?"

"Nothing, I am doing it voluntarily for the Lord." I replied.

At this he burst out laughing. That was the end of Daniel for me. I mention it because the unscrupulous works of some people just drive me mad and I no longer wanted anything to do with him.

Although the men had not returned, Rita and I went up to our room. Long brocade curtains hung at the windows and there was a matching bedcover. The sheets were a brownish white colour, a bit like calico. We just didn't care about the foisty smell we simply jumped into bed and fell asleep.

We woke early on the Saturday morning, refreshed from our sleep. The lorry was back so we assumed the menfolk were still sleeping. We were still hungry so went down to the dining area where this time I could smell coffee. The waiter came over to offer the coffee,

"Da," I responded. (Romanian for yes)

When I saw the coffee in a tiny cup I quickly retracted, it looked like thick tar.

"Nu." (No).

We waited for a while until the men got up so that we could discuss the next stage of our journey. They told us of their exploits down in the town. John Y said that the place looked bleak. There were people everywhere, some queued for bread, others were gathering bits of wood to make fires and there were many people who were literally living on the streets. He said they had parked the van and got out thinking that they would join the queue for bread, but they were foreigners and the people knew it. All eyes were upon them and they felt a bit spooked. He was afraid to leave the van and got back into the cab. A man approached them who could speak English and asked if he could help. John explained that they were looking for some food. The man took them back to his house where there was a lovely smell of cooking. They were given a meal of vegetables, bread, and a glass of wine. They stayed there until the early hours of the morning, obviously forgetting that they had left two hungry women back at the hotel. When they did return we women were asleep in bed. We can only say that once again the Lord had sent His angels to watch over us.

Honoured Guests

We got up early the next morning to go to church at John Pop's invitation. It was situated in another part of Cluj. As we drove up the hill towards the church, we passed streams of people walking up the hill. The men wore suits and hats, the women had long clothes with scarves covering their heads. It was a wonderful sight to see so many people going to that church. By the time we had parked our vehicle we were the last ones to arrive. On leaving the lorry I was still very conscious that we were in Romania and everything we had could be stolen. We had left the other lorry in the hotel's carpark. Again, as a young Christian I didn't trust fully in God's protection, I still trusted my own natural instinct and sensibility.

The service wouldn't start until we arrived. The pastors were waiting outside for us. The church itself looked more like a cathedral. Rita, the two Johns and I were ushered along the aisle to the front and then up steps on the left-hand side into a gallery where we overlooked the whole congregation. We did not expect this or even want it and we were definitely not dressed in the right attire for such an occasion. At least Rita and I wore skirts and head scarves.

Of course we could not understand what the pastors were saying as they led the congregation in praise and prayer.

I must mention here that when the men and women prayed to God they literally cried. Visible streams of tears came down their faces. The women brought out handkerchiefs to wipe their eyes. This apparently shows the depth of love one has for the Saviour. After singing some praises to God the congregation went quiet. John Pop asked us, in English, if we would stand up. We did not understand what was said next but then our names were shouted out one at a time and the people looked up at us and clapped very loudly. We found this very embarrassing. We didn't know that we were going to be presented as special. We definitely didn't want to be in that position, but the Romanian people were honouring us, and they were very prim and proper people with a lot of etiquette. Rita and I were even more embarrassed when the men from the congregation all kissed our hands as we left.

A lady called Maria (a common name as Romanians are mainly Orthodox Catholics) and her daughter Dorina approached us and invited us back to her apartment for lunch. Fortunately Dorina spoke good English and was able to translate for Maria. She didn't have a car and said we would have to go by trolley bus as their apartment was at the other side of the city. The two Johns declined the invitation and said they would go back to the other lorry. Believing both would be safe now, Rita and I went on the trolley bus. What a little adventure. The journey took us an hour. Maria insisted on paying the fare. We enjoyed looking out of the windows at the city buildings. The apartments were huge communist-like buildings, very drab on the outside and identified by large numbers painted on the walls. There seemed to be hundreds of these buildings, it was definitely high-rise living.

We went about fourteen floors up in a lift before arriving at Maria's apartment. We entered through a wooden door and found ourselves in the flat comprising of a small living room, a tiny galley kitchen, a bedroom and a compact bathroom and toilet. Everything was neat and tidy, nothing was out of place.

Both Maria and Dorina were dressed very nicely, unlike the people we had seen in the streets. I thought that maybe the Christian people were blessed and better off than the people on the streets, well this was my way of thinking as a young believer. How naïve!

Dorina, Mel and Maria

Maria laid a little table with a cloth on which she placed china cups and saucers. She prepared a modest lunch for us comprising of Romanian crusty bread, a small portion of Gouda cheese, Spam, tomatoes and gherkins. We were so grateful to share this meal with them. Dorina told us that her mother was a widow, but she had a little clerical job for the local government. She herself didn't have a job, although she was well-educated, as there were no jobs to be had. For one thing there was no money to pay wages at that time. The president had been assassinated, they had been under tight Communist rule and the whole country was in chaos, drained of money through corrupt administration and there wasn't any money in the banks.

She was offering me an insight into what was really going on in this country. My heart was moved and humbled as I thought of how she had put this lunch on for us. The Spam, a processed pork/ham meat, had come from a tin, and she went on to explain that they had a secret allotment where they grew peppers, string beans, tomatoes and onions. That's how she could provide us with a lunch. Once again I felt humbled by the way she had honoured us by showing us hospitality even though she had so little. After long conversations we realized it was evening time. We said our farewells with hugs, kisses and tears and blessed them with a few pounds to help them on their way. I was now beginning to realize that poverty comes in many ways. Although they were not like the people on the streets, they had no money, and no food- that is POVERTY.

I was learning a lot of lessons on this journey. It was bringing home to me how wealthy we were, even though we lived in a gypsy caravan in Bolton. We had never been so poor that we had no food or money, for the outsider looking in on a gypsy site, we would have been classed as poor, in poverty and low life. In reality we had full and plenty.

They insisted that they took us to the trolley bus stop and escorted us back to the hotel where we were able to give them gifts of tin food. They were so happy and cried again as we said our farewells not knowing if we would ever see each other again

Brief encounters with people of God like Maria and Dorina have impacted my life up to this present day. The fact was that they had so very little yet gave us their all. I was beginning to feel very blessed by the depth of love and hospitality that these two Christian women had shown to us.

Chapter 6

Deserted

The two Johns were no-where to be seen when we arrived back at the Hotel Transylvania. It was around eight o'clock when John Y arrived back alone. He told us that John C had met up with some Americans who had also brought aid over and were doing church work. John C told John Y that God had said he should join the Americans. I was quite taken aback because I felt responsible for everyone and I had already explained that we were a team and no-one was to leave each other unless we informed them of a perfectly good reason. Thinking that he would return in the morning we went to bed.

Rita, John Y and I were of the travelling community so we knew each other's ways and instinctively knew what the other would or wouldn't do. John C had no idea of traveller's culture and how the men look after their women. He had come on this journey with just a five pound note in his pocket. He was a Christian man, he could play the guitar and write lovely songs so I said yes he could come with us as he could keep John Y company on this long journey. He had some unusual ways but his heart was good so I could deal with them, but abandoning the ship, walking out on a mission because he had found something better, saying that God had said, just didn't go down well with me. We were a team, two men and two women, and now one man had gone a.w.o.l. My stance on this was that if he didn't come back we would continue the mission without him.

The next morning, Monday, we were up early and packed our bags again ready to head to our next destination, which was Arad, located about 270km south west of Cluj-na-poca. I was to meet a lady doctor called Lydia at the consulate. It had been arranged by Pastor Goos Vedder. We would drop off some medical supplies. After we had had this meeting another lady called Dana took us to her apartment where we were able to have a bath or shower and a meal. The weather was still very hot, in the high thirties, so a bath or shower was much appreciated. These everyday things we take for granted, we learned to appreciate. Dana couldn't speak English so there was little conversation, but her actions spoke of love and kindness in entertaining strangers. Jesus said,

"For whatever you did for one of the least of my brothers and sisters, you did for me." (Matt.25 v.40)

We stayed at Dana's apartment overnight and returned to the consulate the next morning.

Copsa Mica

People were telling us about a village called Copsa Mica (The Black Town). It is about 345 km east of Arad. It was not on my schedule to go there, but after I heard about it, I desperately wanted to go. The big lorry was now almost empty and would be safely guarded at the consulate. John C had not returned so Rita, John Y and I could travel in my lorry. We three would stick together and go off on this new adventure to the Black Town. At the consulate they had actually shown us pictures of the town, overshadowed by a very large factory that oozed out great billows of black poisonous smoke. The pollution covered this town in black soot. I can only believe now that the Lord led me there. I never did take the easy route of anything in my life. I was always the person who was up for a challenge even before I became a Christian. I'd feel happy if I had overthrown something or achieved something or gone where other people wouldn't dream of going. This was yet another challenge for me as I was to find out.

We all felt very happy and united being together in that cab. This lorry was still loaded with clothes and food and now I could give it out liberally as I saw fit. We drove joyfully along the dirt track roads. I now had a map of Romania purchased from one of the garages where I had fuelled up. Did I ever mention

70

that we never paid for any fuel along the way in Romania? Such is the Lord's provision. I checked the map to see how close we were to Copsa Mica and when we got to within two or three kilometres I decided that I would go and investigate first. I didn't know how I was going to do this but one thing I had already learned was that I certainly looked Romanian with my olive skin and dark hair. I drove the lorry to the outskirts of the town and enquired where I would find the mayor (I had a piece of paper with that question written on it in Romanian). The man at the consulate had told me to go to the mayor's office in Copsa Mica. Fortunately it was just five minutes away. We set off, noticing that all the roofs of the houses were black, the grass was black, the railings of the houses were black, the pavements were black, in fact everything was black including a naked and starving little boy to whom we gave bread.

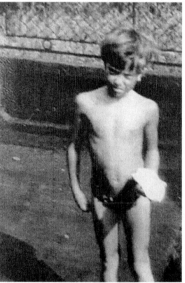

Starving boy

I could see billows of thick black smoke coming out of tall factory chimneys, it dominated the sky but the fall-out came right over

71

the whole town. Copsa Mica was the most polluted town in Romania caused by two large industrial plants, one making carbon black for dyes and the other a smelter. This caused lead poisoning and lung cancer, (Wiki.2017).

The Factory at Copsa mica

We parked the lorry a little way from the town hall. Having changed my mind, I asked Rita to stay with the lorry and told John to come with me in case I got into difficulty. This time I was wearing a long skirt and a headscarf so I would blend in and look less like a stranger. I walked boldly into the mayor's office thinking I would get the last of my aid delivered, in this darkest of places. It would be done very correctly through the mayor, who had the capacity to then distribute it to the poorest people in his town. Oh how naïve I was!

In the mayor's office were four men in blue military style uniforms and two Romanian ladies who I assumed were secretaries or officials. A man with fair complexion was arguing with one of the uniformed officers. He had a deep Scottish accent. They had a translator, a man, who was at his wits end and stuck in the middle of this disagreement. John nor I had spoken a word up to this point. Nobody had taken any notice of us, probably thinking I was just some Romanian. When the Scotsman was shouting angrily, he was swearing using the "f" word, so I intervened,

"Could you please stop using such foul language and can I be of help? What is your problem?"

Well, everyone stopped their arguing and conversations and looked in amazement at John and I because we had spoken in English. The Scotsman was astounded as was everyone else.

"Who the f…. are you?" He rudely questioned.

Follow me

I spoke to him calmly and introduced John and myself as aid workers who had come with aid for the people of the town. The uniformed Romanians looked on in sheer shock as they observed the conversation between the Scotsman and the Romanian looking woman who spoke in her very best English.

"Hello, my name is Melanie Price, does anyone speak English?"

I looked at the mayor and his uniformed aids. The mayor was dressed in a uniform too. He stuck out his arm and pointed across the room with authority at someone or something. I was not sure what. Immediately the Scotsman opened his mouth and with his Scottish accent spoke to me,

"I'm Benny and ya better get outa here right quick hen, they're all bandits and will take everything you have and sell it through the back door on the Black Market."

He had forgotten that one of the Romanian men was a translator and had understood everything he had just said. John and I made a rapid exit through the door. Benny continued to shout at the mayor. We ran out of the entrance door to the street then towards the lorry. Benny was close behind. We ran and ran. Benny called after me,

"Follow me, hen, follow me,"
He climbed into his transit van and John and I jumped into the lorry. We followed them hastily out of the town and turned off down a side lane where we parked up in a furrowed field behind a hedge.

Evening with the McCanns

By now it was getting dark. Benny introduced us to his wife and co-driver and suggested that he and John make a fire to cook on but I preferred to use my Gaz stove. I didn't think making a fire was a good plan really as we didn't want to attract any attention. Meanwhile Rita and I began to talk to Maureen, Benny's wife. She said they were from the west coast of Scotland. They had also seen the plight of the Romanian orphans on the television and had started fundraising and collecting vitamins, educational supplies and clothing. They wanted to bring it out themselves so that they knew that the people

74

actually received the aid. Maureen was a petite woman who seemed quite fragile. She went on to tell us that she had cancer. We were a bit shocked and wondered why she came after being so ill. She said that she wanted to do something to help others before she died.

By now I had set up the Gaz stove as I was really hungry. After frying a few flat chips and some beans we sat around the fire. John and Benny were getting on famously, laughing and chatting and then I discovered why. John Y blurted out that Benny was his father's second cousin. John's family, the Youngs were all in Scotland and some of his aunts had married McCanns who were from Ireland. It's such a small world. This may have been one of my first encounters in which I acknowledged, 'God is in this.' I was amazed at the statistics of this, to be out and about in the heart of Romania, moreover to be in a small town, and John meets his relatives. It was an absolute miracle, after all how many people are in the world?

I have since had many similar experiences over the years of people being related to or knowing one another and meeting in unusual circumstances. For instance, Rita and I were on a ship in the Mediterranean en route to Alexandria in Egypt. Rita got talking to a man and his wife. They enquired of each other where they were from. They were from a town in the north of England near Nelson. Since Rita has a broad northern accent they randomly asked if she knew the Price family. Rita promptly said, "Yes, one of them is here with me".
This man turned out to be my brother-in-law's golfing friend!

The evening was still hot and humid as we shared our meal and had a good conversation. Our bellies were full and the day had been well spent. Rita was the first to admit she was tired and wanted to go to sleep. I went to the back of the lorry and shuffled some boxes and clothing around to make her a bed. Feeling content that I had made her comfortable I returned Benny and Maureen and we talked some more. We discussed what we would do on the morrow as we would be going our separate ways. We decided that we would go back to Copsa Mica and give the clothes out liberally as we saw the need.

The return

Suddenly a piercing scream filled the air. It came from the back of the lorry. Rita…. I knew something had happened to her. Quickly we all ran to the back of the lorry. Poor Rita was beside herself, sobbing hysterically,
"Somebody grabbed me," she wailed.
Disappearing in the distance we heard the tinkling of bells like those the people put on their horse's harnesses. You couldn't hear horse's hooves because the people couldn't afford horse shoes and also they were walking on soft earth. We concluded that some poor man had seized the moment to help himself to some clothes but as it was almost dark, he had grabbed Rita's leg instead. The man was probably as startled as Rita. Needless to say she refused to sleep there again, so John volunteered whilst Rita and I huddled in the cab. We planned to leave at the break of dawn before any other people saw us.

We woke around five. No-one spoke and we didn't eat. We watched the mist rising out of the ground, such a phenomenon. We drove along the dirt track and onto the road to Copsa mica. Here we found some people, who could speak English, and asked where the community centre was. After searching diligently we arrived. The entrance to it was an archway on an elevated slope. I decided to reverse the lorry up and block the entrance so that the back of the lorry was just through the arch and we could deliver the clothing to the centre without anyone hindering us. People had already begun to gather and were guiding me back towards the community hall. I soon realized to my dismay that you can't fit a square peg into a round hole, or should I say the square back of the lorry into an archway. In my excitement to make the delivery of clothes I badly damaged the archway and lost the two rear corners of the lorry. Oh dear! When I saw the damage my heart nearly failed me. The lorry was a hire vehicle and I had had to pay a large deposit on it as it was going on a high risk journey. It was insured but I was now thinking about the excess I would have to pay. It was in this last part of the journey that fear set in. I panicked a little and when I panic, Rita panics. It was really quite selfish because I was focussed on the damage and the fact that I would lose my money.

After a few minutes I saw queues of people either side of the lorry.

Distributing aid in Copsa Mica

They were coming in their droves hoping for a hand-out whereas I wanted to distribute them from the community centre, which indeed we did. But then, I was filled with compassion for those who had come along the street and were beside the lorry. When the lorry was almost empty I decided to let the people help themselves to what was left. I pulled the lorry forward and beckoned to those people to come. They gratefully received all that was placed into their hands. As John was in the back of the lorry the people were saying,

"Multumesc, multumesc." (thank you, thank you).
They were so happy and if they were happy, then I was happy.
To see their smiley faces was worth everything we had been through. We had made these people happy and now I felt that the mission was accomplished. Now the only thing left was the return journey home.

Where is John?

We still had to go back to Arad and pick up the other lorry and hopefully John C. We drove until evening then stopped in a lay-by. Thank God for lay-bys. Out came the faithful gaz stove and we cooked what was left of the potatoes and beans, then rested for a few hours before setting off again. We arrived in Arad by mid-day and went back to the consulate to enquire about our friend and co-worker. Was he there? Apparently no-one had seen him. We asked the uniformed guards who had been guarding the lorry for us but he was nowhere to be found. I started to get worried and then angry and decided that I would have to go on with or without him as I had a deadline to catch the ferry.

My decision to leave was half hearted, on one hand I was angry with John C but on the other my compassion didn't want to leave him behind. There were three of us and only one of him so I asked the security guards if they would make some enquiries to see if anyone knew the whereabouts of the English man. The young guards could see the anguish on my face and said that when they found him they would shoot him! I begged them not to. I would be leaving in half an hour.

As we were about to pull away John C arrived. He was hanging out of an old Cadillac type car which was full of people.
"Wait, wait," he yelled.
He was dressed in khaki shorts and a tee-shirt with 'Jesus loves me' on the front.
"Wait for me," he shouted.

On seeing him I was feeling even more cross because he had deserted the team. He got into the lorry with John Y. As for me, I had steam coming out of my ears and nose like a raging bull but trying to remind myself that the bible says,

"Keep your temper under control, it is foolish to harbour a grudge." (Ecc. 7 v.9)

It really was a good job that he was in the other lorry or I might just have whacked him! Keeping your peace at all times is a hard lesson to learn!

So off we set driving for a while. At the first opportunity we stopped to cook some food, it wasn't much as most of the supplies had gone. It was the first chance I had to speak to John C and ask him where he had been and why?

"Well God told me to go off with the Americans," he innocently replied.

Hmm I thought, God told him! I was not convinced, more likely it was he could play a guitar and sing songs. He went on to say that he had been doing some evangelism and the Americans had given him ten pounds. So he was now financially richer than when he came. Oh dear, John had such a childlike manner so it was easier to forgive him than I thought. He had obviously enjoyed himself so what could I say. We started to laugh about the fact that the security guards were going to shoot him and how I had begged them not to. It could have been serious.

We shared with him about Copsa Mica and what he had missed. I also reminded him that when you are a team you stay together. A team means togetherness. He apologised and we got back to talking about the route home. Out came my European map and pointed out a road higher up than the E80 which we had come on. Most of our money had gone, just enough for fuel and road tolls. We had not paid for fuel in Romania, so we had to be very careful. At least the lorries were now empty and we could drive a little faster. I managed to puncture a rear tyre so I was down to five wheels in Austria. Fortunately the lorry had 4 wheels at the back, but then a further puncture in the other rear tyre in Germany meant that I was down to four wheels. We pressed on with an occasional stop for food or a drink until we arrived to catch the ferry in good time. We must have slept for hours on the way back so we were refreshed for the drive back to Bury.

We had nothing to declare so we came straight through customs then it was the long drive home. As we approached Manchester I heard a loud bang. A tyre had burst. Well I wasn't stopping so I drove the lorry the rest of the way on three tyres. What a miracle. I had left Bury van hire with six tyres and arrived back with three. I explained what had happened to the manager of the hire firm and said he didn't care as he was in awe of the fact that we had completed our mission. He was quite emotional at our achievement. So we had come to the end of the journey.
MISSION ACCOMPLISHED.

Aftermath

We said our farewells, then I returned to the little caravan site in Bolton feeling both happy and satisfied. Coming down from the adrenalin high of the adventurous mission, I was wondering, what next?

I couldn't wait to tell everyone about the trip, show the photographs and describe all the experiences. The reality was, back to the grindstone. When I got back to my family, I just couldn't get a word in as they were all telling me about the family news and gossip. By the time I had listened to all that, the desire to share with them about my trip had gone and would probably have fallen on deaf ears. The next day it was all about getting back to work and the cost of being away for two weeks. When I went to church the following Sunday, it was church as normal and not even a few moments to share about the wonderful trip I had just returned from.

This was my very first mission trip and so full of adventures and excitement. I had actually been there and done it! My eyes were opening to how God was with us with every

step and turn of the wheel. It was the beginning of becoming a leader and taking responsibility for other people's lives and the aid we had taken. It gave an insight into the way other people lived and put my own life into perspective. I had seen God's hand move each time I was in trouble and when I called on Him.
"And call upon me in the day of trouble: I will deliver thee, and thou shalt glorify me." (Psalm 50 v 15).

I had learned many lessons and it wasn't long before I craved to go again. Seeing the joy of the people and children receiving the urgently needed supplies was so rewarding. Most of all I was beginning to enjoy this new Christian life I had found. I was still learning how to pray and to call on the name of Jesus and listen to the prompting of the Holy Spirit. Everything was done for Him with Him and by Him, so I give God all the Glory. Amen.

Joe Smith pictured on the right and below by the doorway, ministering to the people in the village

Chapter 7

Gypsy Joe Smith

I quickly fell back into the same old routine, cooking, cleaning and looking after my children who were becoming teenagers.

Johnny was out working with his father every day, Thomas, the eldest, was out working on his own tree cutting business, Mela stayed at home, cleaning and looking after the youngest, little Dino, who was still at school. My other daughter JoJo was also out door to door selling her wares even though she was supposed to be at school. I was still buying and selling containers, drums and pallets. Life was back to how it was, or so I thought. I was so hungry for more of the bible and the reality of knowing more of God. I went to every church meeting there was. My husband, at this time, was becoming backslidden and much preferred the pub to going to church. We became distant from each other.

It was several years later when at one of the gypsy conventions I heard more about a Christian man called Gypsy Joe Smith. Joe was going out to Romania with a lorry of aid and he was smuggling bibles in too. Now I thought to myself, I really should meet this man and find out more about what he was doing and what aid he needed. I found him in Nantwich with his wife and four daughters. I was amazed at what he was doing. He was part of a group of men from Crewe and Stoke on Trent who had a heart to take aid to Romania and preach the gospel. Joe had been driving his lorry out there for many years.

To promote his work he would do illustrated talks in the churches to highlight the needs and conditions of these people. Those who heard would sponsor and donate not just money but household items, medical things, toiletries, food and clothing.

I was well impressed with this man when I first met him. As he would say,
"I am taking the food and the gospel to my own people."
Although Gypsy Joe didn't live in a caravan, his parents and grandparents had lived in caravans and horse drawn wagons.
"Can I come with you next time you go?" I was quick to ask.
After telling him the adventures I had had on my trip Joe said yes, as long as I brought someone with me. His next trip was to be in September.

I WAS SMITTEN, I HAD CAUGHT THE BUG AND WAS RARING TO GO.

The green Mondeo

I left Joe's house feeling very excited. I was learning to ask God for everything I wanted and I WANTED TO GO! I began to prepare for the next trip. I prayed about it to see if it really was God's will. I would go with Joe and he would be providing the finances. Meanwhile I immersed myself in my business. I decided that I needed a new and reliable car to drive to Romania behind Joe in his lorry. I had a friend whose husband bought and sold cars. Recently he had bought a fleet of five Mondeo cars. He too was a young Christian. When I told him that I needed a reliable car he invited me to come and look at the ones he had newly acquired. One was pink, one light blue, one dark blue, one green and one white. Well I was not a pink girl, I didn't really like white and the blue ones were just standard models, so that left the green one. It was a sporty model, with 2000cc turbo diesel engine, low profile wheels and many sporty extras. This was the one for me!! All I had to do now was negotiate a price. I didn't have much in the way of savings in those days even though I was earning good money with my oil drum collections. In my mind I had an amount of how much I was willing to pay, then I prayed, please Lord give me the car. When I told him what I wanted the car for he was astonished that I, a woman, would even be thinking such things. He said he would sell me the car for the exact amount that he had paid for it and I was so happy when the amount he asked for was the amount that I was prepared to pay. Now I had my car for taking the long journey

When I told the family that I was to embark on another trip and I was going to drive my newly acquired car they again thought I was crazy. They said that the car would come back battered and broken because it was a wild country with poor roads that I was heading to. I told them that the Lord had provided this vehicle for such a journey as this and that it was only a piece of metal after all.

My little friend Rita asked if she could come along with me. I said yes immediately. She had enjoyed the last trip and the adventure of it all. Joe had rung and asked if I had room in my car for three more people so I said yes. It might be a squeeze but it meant that we would share the fuel costs and expenses. Now I could see that God was putting together a team of dedicated people who were giving time, money and efforts to fulfil the calling of God in their lives. Ken and Muriel were from churches in Colwyn Bay in Wales. Muriel had been doing beach evangelism along the coasts of Wales so the team members had some experience beforehand. The fifth passenger was Eddie Bracegirdle from White Hill Methodist church, Stoke on Trent.

Departure

The day dawned when we were to leave on our journey. We all met up in Nantwich. Joe had not only his own high-topped transit van loaded with aid but also two other volunteers driving a very big lorry filled with everything that would be useful for the recent church plants in Romania such as Dorohoi. My new Mondeo was a nice car to drive and so much easier than the lorry on my first trip. I could put it into fifth gear with cruise control. Joe, the leader of this team had given us an outline map with the route so we all knew where we were going. It was intended that I would follow the lorry as it was full and couldn't go too fast. This made it easier for me driving my car and I was able to have lovely conversations and fellowship with my travelling companions, Ken, Muriel, Rita and Eddie.

Our basic maps!!

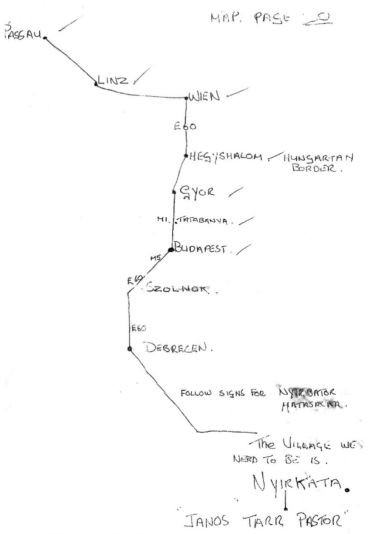

MAP. PAGE 2

PASSAU.

LINZ

WIEN

E60

HEGYSHALOM . HUNGARIAN BORDER.

GYOR

M1. TATABANYA .

BUDAPEST .

M5

E60 SZOLNOK .

E60

DEBRECEN .

FOLLOW SIGNS FOR NYIRBATOR HATASARKTA .

The VILLAGE WE NEED TO BE IS .

NYIRKATA.

JANOS TARR PASTOR

We arrived in Dover then crossed to Ostend without a hitch, then into Germany where we stayed with a Christian brother called Gunter and his family overnight. We set off early the next morning after breakfast, continuing on through Germany and into Austria where we stayed in a panzio. The next day was another early start and we drove through Austria and

87

Hungary where we stayed overnight in Sylvia's panzio (guest house) in Tata. The weather was very hot and I thanked God for air conditioning in my new car. The men driving the lorries had no such luxury. As we drove I noticed things that were familiar to me from my first trip. I felt more relaxed driving the car and not being the leader. Now I was part of a team. I could enjoy the scenery as it changed from one country to another. It was surprising how many kilometres we travelled in a day on the E80. It's so easy to drive on one straight road journeying west to east.

Arriving in Hungary again brought excitement back to me especially when I saw the signs to Budapest. My heart longed to see this fairy-tale city again, but obviously I had to stay on this autobahn to keep up with the lorries. I consider myself a faithful follower and good team member. It was so nice having a man making all the decisions and knowing what he was doing. It was a lesson I have never forgotten because to be a leader you first have to be a follower. There were certain rules that Joe had laid down. We were not to overtake nor stop without flashing the lorries to let them know, nor were we to go off with anyone without telling Joe.

We passed by Budapest and Joe headed for the second largest city, Debrecen, which took us over six hours. Then we took a south easterly direction to the village of Nyirbeltek. Again we passed through many villages, all looking exactly the same.

Dani and Kati

Dani and Kati.

Nyirbeltek sits on the Romanian border and we were going to spend the night here in a Roma village in the home of Dani and Kati Beri. They were extremely poor and had two children, a boy called Dani junior and a girl called Szuika. They lived in a little mud brick house which looked as though it could barely stand, but it had a big garden where they grew vegetables. They kept a pig in a sty and had chickens running around. We parked the van and the car here, the lorries had to remain out on the road. Immediately as I got out of the car, I saw a lovely little woman with a big smile on her face shouting repeatedly, "Hello, hello."

She had fair skin, a round broad face and the most beautiful slanted blue eyes I had ever seen, glistening with joy to see us. Her brownish blonde hair framed her face and fell neatly on her shoulders. She was wearing a simple A-line dress covered by a pinafore which suggested that she had been cooking. Oh, we were very hungry!! We hadn't stopped in any of the villages for food as Joe said we had to continue until nightfall. It was now dusk and all we wanted was food and sleep. Kati invited us into her humble home. The furniture, even though it looked like it might collapse at any time, was spotlessly clean. The smell of Hungarian goulash was coming from a huge cauldron which was set over an open fire outside. It was a heavenly smell. It was ironic that we had come to feed the poor and yet here were the poor feeding us.

Little did I know that this first meal that Kati had cooked was going to be the beginning of a wonderful and Godly friendship which would become an international ministry that would reach to the far east of China and Taiwan. Talk about humble beginnings! You couldn't get any more humble than this. There was a table and four chairs in the room and we ladies were invited to sit down as she served us with this amazing meal. Meanwhile the men ate their portions outside chatting happily. They were pleased that at long last they had arrived at this tiny village.

After the meal and our thank you (Koszonom), Kati showed us where we would sleep. The living room and kitchen were all one room and the front room was Dani and Kati's bedroom which looked out onto the tiny dirt track road where horses and carts passed by. The kitchen comprised of a stove with a metal chimney up to the roof and a little table with aluminium bowls for preparing food and washing up in. There was no running water in the house nor was there a toilet. The latter was housed in a wooden hut at the end of the garden and consisted of a piece of wood with a hole in it. Your business would go through the hole into the ground and be absorbed by the soil. I later discovered that they would move the toilet hut to a different location in the garden from time to time and leave a stick to mark where it had been so that it wouldn't be used again for a year. I have to say they had the best carrots and onions I have ever tasted!!

Our sleeping quarters consisted of one small room split by a curtain. Rita and I shared a single bed where we slept head to toe. There were two boards on four stilts where Ken and Muriel slept. The mattress was a blanket folded and placed inside a cover. We had single sheets to cover us. The weather was hot anyway. Hey ho, this was a taste of mission hospitality at its basic and I was in training. All exhausted we soon fell asleep and only woke the next morning around six to hear the cockerel crowing. After our breakfast of fresh eggs and home-made bread we were off, our destination was Petrosani in Romania.

Joe the preacher

We were full of enthusiasm and anticipation as we got into our various vehicles and hit the road. Before heading to Petrosani Joe took us to Nyirkata, a neighbouring village, to do some street evangelism. When Joe stepped out of his big van, the people were already gathering. They had heard the engines of western lorries approaching. He immediately started preaching the gospel in a very loud voice. He had the ability to project his voice so even those at the back could hear.

Nyirkata is a village known to Joe, he had been there once before to preach. He had met Ferri who became his Hungarian translator and who spoke very good English. His father was called Frank and he was the pastor of a church in Mateszalker. Ferri was living in Nyirkata and was caring for a lovely old pastor called Janos. Janos had fled to Australia from Hungary in the times of the troubles when the Hungarian Peoples Republic was rebelling against Russian rule in 1956. Janos had learned to speak English while he was there. Latterly he had been able to teach Ferri to speak English, so he was able to translate for Joe.

Joe very vehemently preached the gospel under the power of the Holy Spirit. We were all amazed to see this different side of Gypsy Joe as he was quite a calm, quiet and reserved man. Here he was shouting loudly into the crowds which were now forming. He spoke about the love of Jesus.

The children gawped with big, wide eyes and were open mouthed in astonishment. The women and girls were nodding their heads in agreement with what he was saying. Now this was all new to me, and I was absolutely in awe when I saw people coming forwards for prayer, crying and repentant.

By now the men of the village had come over too. I was aghast as I saw Joe calling them forward and telling them that they were the children of the Most High God who loved them so very much. He told them that God wanted them to turn their lives round, to stop doing wicked things and start living a righteous life for Jesus. It was my earliest experience, and a good one I may add, of the real meaning of evangelism with love and yet authority.

Chapter 8

Something miraculous

As I write, I am back there with the crowds and the dogs running round barking. The whole scene was powerful and fuelled by something. In those days I thought it was the power of Gypsy Joe. It took several years to realize that this was the power of the Holy Spirit with the truth of the words of the gospel coming together to bring salvation to those who were listening. Now what did all that mean? Were we going to raise an army and start a revolution? No. Joe continued to call the people forth and to repent of their wicked ways (sins) which had brought poverty, sickness and darkness into their lives. God had sent His servants to bring in the light that would show them the way back to God in love and righteousness.

Now I must tell you, the reader, that these words were relatively new to me. Repentance, salvation, sin, but I was learning quickly and I was very excited about it all. Joe went on to explain that hunger, poverty, lawlessness, fighting, feuding, stealing and lying were not from God. Therefore it had to be another source and that source was the evil one, the devil, who had influenced their lives so much that they had become addicted to this way of life. Joe continued, the wages of sin is death and it is the death of one's own soul, salvation means the saving of that soul. He told them to repent which means stopping the sin, turning around from your old life and asking God to forgive you of all your wrong doings and start afresh. He said this can only be done through Jesus Christ. He went on to quote John 3 v.16 from the bible,

"For God so loved the world that He gave His only begotten son that whosoever believes in Him shall not perish but have eternal life."

He told them that Jesus died on the cross at Calvary for every one of us. By this time Joe was becoming very emotional and his voice had lowered as he told his listeners, both young and old, that God sent Jesus His son to pay the price for our sins. God sent Him to earth to be cruelly whipped and slaughtered in our place, so we could be forgiven. Joe had taken a handkerchief from his pocket and was wiping his brow. The air was so charged with emotion that the people started to weep. None of us really knew what was happening but something very powerful was moving the people. The crowd had swelled to more than a hundred who were listening and responding. They started to cry out,
"God help us. Jesus help us. We are sorry for our selfish and Godless ways."

Some of the people knelt down and most of the women were wiping their tears and noses on their scarves. We were all crying, even me. Joe lifted his hand and beckoned the people to come forward and give their lives to Jesus. The people flooded forward. Joe through Ferri, the interpreter, led them corporately in a prayer, first proclaiming Jesus Christ as Lord, Jesus Christ son of God, and Jesus Christ who is God. He went on to lead them in a prayer asking God for forgiveness for all their wrong doings, their wrong attitudes, their ignorance of God and His ways. The people were not just saying these words they were wailing them out in true repentance. As they cried out, the Holy Spirit of God moved and the people knew that their sins had been washed away. They knew that they had been made new after Joe had prayed this prayer. I do not know how many people gave their lives to the Lord that day but something miraculous had happened.

All of this had been translated by Ferri, but now he was speaking directly to the people himself. Ken and Muriel were giving out tracts written in Hungarian. Joe continued his ministry by giving out a plea for those who were sick to come forward and he would pray for them individually. The emaciated young

94

women came first with babies in slings or toddlers astride their hips. Many old ladies dressed in black (showing that they were widows or recently bereaved) came forward. The men came last with sombre faces, rubbing their body to indicate what their ailment was. I didn't know what to pray or how to pray for them. I didn't have the courage to pray aloud when I was alone or with others. That was to come later.

Ferri started to sing as he played his guitar. I couldn't understand the words but in one moment it seemed that the people dried their eyes and were singing along with him. It must have been a well-known song as they opened their mouths and sang with no inhibitions and an abundance of joy in their hearts. Little did I know that I was being taught and shown how to evangelise, to preach the gospel and to do ministry by leading the people to the Lord. I can now say that I have probably ministered to thousands after thirty years or more of ministry. Those early days were my training ground.

Joe gestured to one of the lorry drivers to bring some bags of clothes out of the van. Big John (called because of his height) threw four large black bags onto the ground in the midst of them. I expected the people to rush forward and tear the bags apart, but they didn't. They simply stood and stared at the bags. Rita, Muriel and I started distributing the children's clothing out liberally. The ladies were so happy. The dark, rugged faced men looked happy but concerned themselves with getting out their cigarettes. It seemed that everyone smoked, even some of the younger boys. I was shocked but pretended not to be. This was a very good days' work. We had given clothes, shoes and sweets but more importantly we gave them Christ Jesus. Everyone took a tract and some came back for another one to pass on to relatives.

We were invited to Pastor Janos's house for refreshments. It was the first time I had met him. I saw a very frail looking man reclining on a couch. He was quite fair, with wisps of grey hair. When he saw us he cried out with glee, "Aldott legyen az Ur" (Bless the Lord.)

His tiny turquoise-blue eyes were slanted and squint but they lit up. A force within him was emitting a light that was not natural. Then he spoke in English,

"Welcome my friends, thank you for coming."

Although he was a true Hungarian man, he spoke English with a hint of an Australian accent. He asked some of the people in the house to serve us with apple juice and dry bread with salami and capsicum pepper on the top. While we ate he told us the story of his escape from Hungary to Australia who accepted exiles, and how he had learned to speak English.

Into Romania

Refreshed, and after lots of farewells and blessings given and received, we boarded our vehicles and set out to cross into Romania before nightfall. It was quite easy as we were not too far from the border at Oradea. All three vehicles crossed as a convoy easily and with no problems. Joe had crossed that way before.

Now we were set for hours of driving into this extraordinary, beautiful nation. Once again entering Romania there was a completely different atmosphere and a different landscape. We had to drive up the side of a big mountain, the van and lorry chugged up slowly and I had to drop down to third or second gear to drive up and to make sure I stayed behind the lorry. My sporty Mondeo could have sped up like road-runner but Ken, Muriel, Rita and I were having such wonderful conversations about what had happened in Nyirkata. I was happy to just drive sedately behind.

At one stage as we neared the top of the mountain we ladies urgently needed a toilet stop. We were driving along a single track road, flanked by forest and with no sign of life. It was getting increasingly dark, so I flashed my lights to the other vehicles to slow down as I needed to stop. Joe pulled into a passing place and we ladies ran quickly from the car to the seclusion of the forest where we could pee in private. The men politely turned their heads until we returned. Then it was their turn to water the trees! When we gathered back at the vehicles the men gestured to get into the car with some urgency because in our desperation we had not seen the sign. It showed a picture of a bear and written in Romanian said, "Attentie la Urs" warning us of bears. Romanian bears are brown grizzlies and are notorious for being vicious.

We returned to the car hastily and took off at speed. I think I would have liked to see a bear but considering our health and safety it was better that we didn't. I did however see one later in a Romanian village where we stopped to look at some sort of festival or fair. I saw a man with a bear on a chain, not a big grizzly one but when it stood on its back legs it was taller than the man. It was a dancing bear. It was like turning the clock back hundreds of years into history. There were jugglers, a merry-go-round, people selling flowers and sweetmeats. We didn't stop to look round properly as we were on a timescale and needed to keep moving.

As far as I remember we drove all through the night until we reached Petrosiani in the early morning, it was dawn and shrouded in mist. Everywhere looked shabby, poor and lifeless at that time of day. We had reached our destination. We met George Dobre, the leaders and two other men from the church. We ladies were escorted to a small flat where we were going to sleep. Petrosiani is a mining town situated on a river and at the side of a mountain. The coal mines had closed down just like it was happening in Wales in the UK. In this town there was no work left of this nature. Joe and the men would sleep in the vehicles as it was too dangerous to leave them unattended. For one thing the Russian Mafia were closing in as they do when they see a town or a village that is vulnerable. If they saw any wealth rising up or coming in they would surely want a slice! The men here still had Kalashnikov rifles and would use them at the bat of an eyelid. So the van and the lorry were hidden at the back of the flats where they were less noticeable.

I sometimes think of the danger we put ourselves in just by bringing aid out because eyes are everywhere and this part of Romania still had to adhere to communist ideals. The people were suspicious of their neighbours let alone strangers coming into the town. Never-the-less here we were, a team of people on a mission to deliver aid to the poor via the church. And that is exactly what we did.

The Little Orphanage

We took some aid to a little orphanage which was a single storey building. There were little scantily dressed toddlers running around. The staff, who were dressed in white uniforms, received us in a very official way, and the director who was a man, thanked us formally as the men unloaded most of the aid from the lorry and the van. The lorry had been driven by Big John who was from Yorkshire. He had a skin complaint on his hands and so he continually wore black leather gloves. I am sure his hands must have been very sore from gripping the steering wheel for so long. His co-driver Little John was from Ely. He lived by the sea with his wife and they fostered children. Joe Smith, Eddie and the two Johns followed the directors into the office for a discussion. We three ladies tried to communicate with the children and staff. The children seemed quite afraid of us and the staff remained official.

We moved on from there to Aninoasa, in the county of Hunedoara, in the region of Transylvania. We were to meet up with Pastor Gregorias, a priest, and his wife who was an ex-nun. They had left the Catholic church and become Born Again Christians. They were now pastors of five Pentecostal churches. What a lovely spiritual man he was. There was such an overwhelming warmth of love and welcoming when they received us. We shared a meal of delicious soup and bread. Their house was close to the church which was at the other side of the courtyard. The men slept in the lorries and the ladies had the luxury of their flat.

As it was now Saturday we were invited to visit their church the very next day. We felt a little nervous. However, we had a good night's sleep and enjoyed a quick wash before attending the service at ten thirty. Oh, how lovely it was to experience those brothers and sisters worshipping and praising the Lord Jesus Christ with a freedom and a reality of knowing their God. There was no holding back in their prayers of thanksgiving in between the praise and worship. About thirty people gathered in the morning and about seventy in the evening. When the pastor spoke to his people it was as a shepherd who loved his sheep. His very demeanour was of love, care and consideration as he encouraged them to believe that God was going to do something to alleviate their poverty. He spoke with authority yet a gentleness reflecting the true love of Christ.

This was now one of my first experiences of speaking to a congregation. The Pastor's son Victor became our translator. I said I was happy to be there, told them my name and a little about my family and that I was a Born Again Christian. I really enjoyed the experience and it was my introduction into speaking publicly to peoples of many nations. At the evening meeting we distributed more clothes and toiletries which I found very rewarding. After another meal and a good night's sleep it was time to head back to England. It's always easier to travel with empty vehicles.

Kati's story

We passed through Nyirbeltek and stopped by again at Dani and Kati's home to be refreshed. Once again Kati was ready for us with more food waiting and a very warm welcome. Since we were not in such a hurry, we were able to find out a little more about her and her family of children and brothers and sisters. This conversation went on to the point where Kati said

99

that she wanted to teach the bible to her children. She explained that some Hungarian speaking Jehovah's Witnesses had visited the village and she had become one of them. They had come into this poor village with something new, something about God. Because she and Dani were seeking God they grasped it all with both hands until one day a ninety year old man, Brother Wilson, from Colwyn Bay in Wales arrived with his wife, called Jenny and a Pastor, Charles Price, who was an American and also living in Colwyn Bay. Brother Wilson shared with them a verse from John 3 v.3. Jesus said,

"Verily, verily, I say unto thee, except a man be born again he cannot see the kingdom of God."

Once again the word of God with the power of the spirit was bringing the truth with freedom and love. Brother Wilson could never speak Hungarian but he expounded the bible verses to Kati. It was quite a miracle as Kati looked up the verses in her bible as Brother Wilson pointed them out in his. The barrier of language was overcome. While he was staying there he became mentor, teacher, pastor, brother and friend. On hearing the teaching both Kati and Dani repented and invited Jesus into their hearts and gave their lives to Christ, they were Born Again. Kati and Dani started to learn English when I visited with them, again using our bibles. We understood each other in the spirit and bit by bit we learned each other's language by the grace of God.

If they had only known at that time that their decision would change the lives of so many people of different nations, they might not have believed it. I can say that because I myself am so enriched by them. We have formed a deep friendship over thirty years. Who would ever have thought that, least of all me? Dani and Kati's village is nearly two thousand miles from my home in the U.K. How could anyone think of having developed a friendship with anyone over this distance? Only God could do this. He gave me such a love for this couple, a real connection of hearts. To this day, thirty years on we remain as one spirit and one heart.

We made it.

We left Nyirbeltek the next day for the long haul back. It was about two days journey with very short stops at service stations for a sandwich and drink. Joe driving the van and the lorry drivers sped on ahead of me as I had my passengers. He knew that I knew where I was going and the ferry time. I was anxious. If I missed it, it would cost me a lot of money to pay for another crossing. In those days I lived on a shoestring. My anxiety was correct, because when I arrived at the port all the lorries and cars were already on and the foot passengers had boarded. I just made it by the skin of my teeth. I had about five minutes to spare and mine was the last vehicle onto the boat. I cannot tell you the relief I felt when I was waved to come on board. It was a fully loaded ferry and I was squeezed in with inches to spare. BUT, I had made it. My lovely Mondeo car had done her job but she was badly battered, just as I had been warned. Goats in Romania had butted their reflections in it, a herd of sheep had walked into it, I had driven along dirt tracks, rocky roads, stone tracks and many times failed to avoid pot holes and the curious children who had left handprints all over it as they begged for food and sweets. BUT WE MADE IT!

After jubilantly getting out of the car we made our way to the restaurant deck where little did I know that the next piece of God's jigsaw puzzle of my life was to be put into place. Had I missed the boat then I would have missed the opportunity to find a missing link with my past, then later encounter the man who was to play a very big role with the missions in my life for the next fifteen years. God's timing is perfect. The story of my early life and the missing link is written in my first book "Shadows of the Rainbow." (2018)

Mr Alex Humphreys (on the right) in front of the lorry

Mr Alex, with the children in the early wood and plastic lean-to church in Nyirbeltek.

Chapter 9

Mr Alex Humphreys

In my first book I wrote about my first encounter with Mr. Alex Humphreys at Knutsford service station on the M6. Mr. Alex Humphreys began to explain that he had recently been in his local library in Stoke on Trent when by chance he bumped into an old school friend called Eddie Bracegirdle. They recognised each other straight away how could they fail to? Mr. Alex stood 6'5" tall and Eddie about 4'10" and they hadn't seen each other for over thirty-five years. Alex gazed at him,

"Is that really you Eddie?"

"Yes Alex, it's me."

Mr. Alex had a way of sniffing in a breath through his nose after almost every sentence. It was like a snort and gave him a kind of posh Potteries accent,

"What are you doing with yourself these days my good fellow?"

"Oh, I have been going out to Romania." Eddie replied.

"What have you been doing out there?"

Eddie explained that he had been helping to take aid and food to the orphans. Mr. Alex replied with a snort,

"That seems a very admirable thing to do. Who do you go with?"

Mr. Alex's interest was stirred as Eddie continued,

"I go out with a man called Gypsy Joe Smith who has been talking to people about the plight of these orphans. He is invited to speak in the local churches around the Stoke area and collects clothes, bric-a-brac and food which people donate. Then he meets up with some other men and they drive ten-ton lorries over to distribute the aid directly to the genuinely needy."

Eddie said he loved going out there even though what he saw was shocking. Mr. Alex's sense of adventure had been awakened.

"Well I think I would like to do something like that. Can we meet up for a coffee and further chat next week?" he enquired.

With that arranged they shook hands and agreed to meet the following Wednesday. It was the beginning of a great adventure for them both. The result of the meeting was that Mr. Alex had a big lorry that he was going to fill it with clothes, toiletries, medicines, sweets, electrical goods, towels, bedding and crockery along with dried and tinned food. He asked Eddie if he could arrange a driver to take it out the next time that Joe Smith was going.

Now Eddie had some very disturbing photographs of the orphanages which he had taken while he was out there. Mr. Alex was moved with compassion for those nearly naked and starving children. And so it was that a few weeks later everything had been collected from Mr. Alex's wholesaler friends. It was only when I got to know Mr. Alex Humphreys better that he told me his own story.

Mr. Alex's story

Following a chance meeting with someone, Mr.Alex was persuaded to plough his available funds into a supermarket that would transform his career and his life. He became the creator of a new money saving concept of supermarket shopping. Instead of making elaborate displays, produce was simply sold from the cardboard boxes stacked on the shelves. He bought from wholesalers and simply added a penny per item. Within two years he would break even and then begin to make a profit. This new shopping experience helped to reduce the number of staff required to run the stores. He rented a small building with shop frontage in Kidsgrove. Out at the front he would display brushes, brooms, shoe polishes and special offers to attract the customers. Inside the other goods were stacked in categories, not only foodstuffs but other household goods as well, making it an easy way to shop both for the customer and the cashier. There was little need for serving staff or elaborate display counters. Everything was paid for at one till. Instead of two years, he began to show a profit after six months.

It was the early 1960's and he brought the concept of the wholesaler into the towns and cities. The C n C supermarket chain was born. It was profitably sold out to Kwik Save supermarkets in 1978. (oatcakefranzine.proboards.com)

Still only aged fifty-two at the time of the sale, Mr. Alex devoted much of his time to charity work. In 1968 he became a director and Life Vice Persident of Stoke City football club In 1995 he was made freeman of the city of Stoke on Trent for his services to charities and businesses. His personal project was creating a holiday home called The Old School in Llangoed, Anglesey, Wales, for handicapped children from the North Staffs area. Once a year he would organise a grand concert at the Victoria Hall in Hanley to fund the upkeep of "The Old School."

Three strangers

Mr. Alex told Eddie that he wasn't going to drive out to Romania and asked him if he would like to fly with him. Eddie said that he preferred to go in the lorries as a co-driver. So Mr. Alex and Eddie went to meet with Gypsy Joe Smith. Joe had been going out to Romania not only taking aid but also evangelising in the poor villages. Mr. Alex asked Joe if he knew of anyone who would accompany him on the flight. Joe gave Mr. Alex three names and I, Melanie, was one of them. This is how I came to receive the phone call from Mr. Alex Humphreys, just eleven days after my second trip to Romania, asking me to meet him at the motorway services. This meeting changed the course of the lives of my family and friends and also that of Mr. Alex Humphreys.

I might just point out that although I have already referred to Mr. Alex Humphreys as Mr. Alex, I had known him for quite a while before I was able to call him Mr. Alex. I had a great respect for this man.

Well, of course after he had asked me to take further aid to Romania, I did what I do now. I prayed, and I also prayed with dear Joan Hanson who was a missionary and had served 30 years in China and Taiwan. Now in her eighties, she was staying with me and came to the meeting with Mr.Alex. The result was that I had the "go ahead" from Father God. Even in those early days I had learned that if I did anything on my own without consulting with my Father God, and in my own strength, that it would not work out. Even today I must know that any mission trip, or as it was then, aid trip, had to have God's blessing on it.

I told Mr. Alex that I would accompany him but we needed a third person to come along with us. Little old me, uneducated and from a scary background could not go alone with a big businessman. So it was that a few days later I received a call from a lady in Leek called Ann who was to become the third person. She was neither a friend of Eddie nor of Mr. Alex but was acquainted with Joe Smith via her church. She was also part of a Christian women's international group. She asked if we could meet up, with a view to going out to Romania for the first time. I was invited to her church and to discuss the possibilities of going.

The following Sunday I was there, speaking and showing photographs of what I had seen and done on my first trip. From that meeting a man offered to pay for my flight. To this day I do not know who he was. I was quite taken aback. It was not in my head that I would ever be able to afford to fly. Now I had to think how this was all going to work out. Ann was a real country lady with a husband and two children, Mr. Alex was a well-known gentleman and businessman who was very bossy and used to shout a lot. I really didn't like him in those early days but I had to deal with it because through him many children in Romania would benefit. You couldn't look a gift horse in the mouth, as they say. I saw that it was God who was using Mr. Alex for His glory. God had sent Mr. Alex into my life and He would give me the ability to deal with him. Ann on the other hand, was a country bumpkin with a sweet, gentle, Christian nature. I really liked her and we got on very well from the moment I met her.

There we were meeting at Manchester airport, three strangers, the farmer's daughter, the supermarket millionaire and moi! Mr. Alex, in his very assertive voice, was demanding a seat with leg room. Ann and I stayed in the background and allowed him to take the lead as we boarded the plane. He seemed to be a little nervous but Ann kept talking about the Lord and how He is always with us wherever we go. The flight was just over two hours. I slept most of the way, Ann read her bible and Mr. Alex read his newspaper.

Culture shock

It was afternoon when we arrived in Budapest, Hungary and we picked up our hire car. I drove the six hours towards the Romanian border. We were going to have a meal and stop overnight in a little Hungarian village, where we had to wait for the lorries to arrive the next day. Then we would continue across the border to deliver the aid from the lorries to the designated orphanage. I followed the route which Joe had given me. We drove east out of Budapest. Not long after leaving the city the tarmac roads turned to dirt tracks. I simply followed the route. We drove through village after village all looking the same. We could hardly tell where one village ended and the next one started. The only way you could tell was the road sign which had a cross through it to indicate you had left. Once again the roadside activity fascinated me, the basket sellers, the horse dealers, people selling livestock and the horses and carts.

Although the road was dusty and the weather hot, the journey wasn't boring as Mr. Alex, Ann and I were beginning to get to know one another a little better. Intermittently we would stop for a coffee and a sandwich and as Mr Alex announced, "Everything is going spiffingly well duckie."
We reached Nyirbeltek around seven o'clock, entering the village again where Kati and Dani lived. It seemed shabby, dusty and

very poor. The old women, traditionally dressed in black and wearing headscarves sat on benches, the children were playing, joined by dogs running around barking, the smell of horses, the pigs snorting and the sounds of chickens continue to delight my senses to this day.

Dani and Kati came out to greet us. Kati was very pleased to see us even though she always seemed to be bustling around to get things done. She was eager for us to sit down for a meal. I was happy to be in Kati's humble abode again. We gestured our thanks to her as we, at that time, could barely speak each other's language, so conversation was limited. Eventually we gestured that we would like to go to bed as we were very tired and it was after ten o'clock.

These poor villages had no street lighting. The street was really a dirt track between clusters of little houses and Dani's house was definitely "off the beaten track." When night time came it really was pitch black and more so in the winter months. Mr Alex was looking a bit drained and tired. I think he had had a bit of a culture shock and considering his age I thought it was best to have an early night ready for the arrival of the lorry drivers the next morning. Kati showed us to the back room which was divided by a curtain. Mr. Alex was to sleep at the latter end in case he needed to get up in the night. He would still have to pass by where Ann and I were sleeping, go through the living room, out through the front door, along the side of the house and past the vegetable patch before arriving at the small wooden shed with the hole in the ground. All of this would have to be done in the pitch black unless you had a torch which of course he didn't. So we all "watered" the garden before turning in and hoped that was it until morning! I wasn't very comfortable on my wooden mattress and was sleeping head to toe with Ann. We were so tired though that we soon drifted off to sleep.

Crisis

It seemed to me that no more than five minutes had passed by when I was disturbed by the sounds of pounding feet and breathlessness coming from Mr. Alex at the other side of the curtain. He was breathing very heavily and then there was a big thud on the floor. I was startled and wondered for a moment where I was. I quickly shouted out,

"Mr. Alex Humphreys are you O.K."

He replied in a deep, gasping breath,

"No duckie, no duckie."

I lit a candle and went behind the curtain to find Mr. Alex in his pyjamas sitting upright and grasping his chest. By this time Ann had come through as well.

"Take me home, take me home, take me back. I have made a big mistake, I should never have come." Mr. Alex was saying.

Ann in a very soothing voice started to reassure him,

"Let's keep calm, calm down Mr.Humphreys you are in a strange place and you will be alright."

Now I, fearing the worst, thought he was having a heart attack. Dani and Kati came to see what was happening.

"Take me back, take me back." Mr. Alex insisted.

By now he had put his head between his legs and his hands on his head. He was still groaning,

"Take me back, take me back, I shouldn't be here."

Kati had brought a glass of water and was speaking to us in Hungarian, we guessed she was saying to give him water. Mr. Alex was insisting that I take him back to the airport in Budapest and right now. At that moment I was more concerned about myself and about the consequences if this man died. Hadn't I brought him out to a poor Roma village in the middle of nowhere?

Here was this big, well-known businessman feeling unwell and I would be to blame if anything happened to him. My mind went into riot mode. It was a six hour drive back to the airport, driving on poor roads in the dark, so I said to him,

"Sir, just let me sleep and rest for an hour or so and I will drive you back to the airport and get you some assistance but then I will be driving back here to continue the mission and deliver the aid to finish what we had started. But, before I do, I am going to pray for you."

So along with Ann, we put our hands on his shoulder as he sat there stressed and dishevelled, and prayed that God would comfort his heart and that he would not take a heart attack, that he would not die but would live and declare the works of the Lord. By now I was beginning to realize that he had not had a heart attack but a panic attack. None of us had any first aid abilities and there wasn't a hospital for miles so no ambulance could be called and there were no mobile phones in those days. Mr. Alex agreed to wait. He took a shot of whiskey from a bottle he had bought at the airport. We helped him to lie down. Ann stroked his arm and spoke some comforting words over him. Then we all returned to try and get some sleep. What could have been a major crisis was averted.

I awoke the next morning not just to the sound of the cock crowing and the birds twittering, but to the sound of Mr. Alex Humphreys yawning very loudly and calling,
"Duckie, what time are those lorry drivers arriving?"
I got up and peeped behind the curtain to see Mr. Alex in his striped pyjamas stretching his arms up into the air, with the biggest smile on his face. Talk about God answering prayer, although for my part it may have been a selfish prayer, God had done it. When he was dressed he went on to eat a hearty breakfast and began to tell us what was going to happen when the lorries arrived. Now Ann, and I, Dani and Kati had found a new man in Mr. Alex. He was now a leader and General. God had restored him. Thank you Jesus.

Beyond belief

As soon as the lorries arrived we set off to the designated orphanage in Romania, a journey of four or five hours. We arrived mid-afternoon and were greeted officially by the director, the head of the nursing staff and a translator. They appeared pleased to see us. We entered the building and climbed a flight of stairs. By now we could hear noises. The smells were getting stronger and as we went into the dormitory my eyes looked in disbelief, utter disbelief, at what I saw. There were about ten or twelve cot-beds and each one had a child in it. I was appalled. I had never before seen human beings in this state, let alone young children. By that I mean they were so emaciated and their bulbous eyes almost seemed to be popping out. I walked over to the first cot and tried to smile at the child. As I put my hand out to touch her she gave a kind of squeal and became very excited, rocking herself backwards and forwards. She looked to be about three or four years old but I was so shocked when I was told she was actually nine years old. I could hardly believe it.

The nurse who was accompanying us happily told me that the children did get three meals a day but didn't say what, so I will never know. She witnessed the disgust on my face when I asked why the child had no hair. The child's head, like the rest of them, was shaved, not a hair in sight. She told us that shaving their heads kept the lice away and it was easier for the nurse to keep them clean. I call her a nurse because she was wearing a uniform but actually the nurses were just child carers.

I approached another child, a little boy, though it was hard to distinguish with their shaven heads. As with the first child, he grunted and let out a squeal of excitement. Once one had started, they all started, making unintelligible noises and rocking back and forth. This little boy was fairer skinned than the others, with blue eyes and fair eyebrows but the sadness on his face was apparent. Basically most of the children were dark skinned with black eyes which I recognised as Roma children. They all wore cloth nappies as they were not allowed out of their cots or toilet trained. In fact they were looked after more like animals.

The scene was exactly as I had watched on the television, those first images. On looking round the room I realized that this was what I came for and this was what the journey was all about. As that thought came into my head, I strengthened myself at the realization that this was the mission and I was actually here fulfilling the call of God on my life to go and feed the orphans. Although still in great shock I kind of knew that I would be back, it wasn't a one-off trip. Something was stirring inside of my spirit as I considered the situation of these poor, abandoned, neglected children. It was the fault of a greedy and evil leader, Ceausescu, who channelled all of the country's wealth into private offshore accounts for himself and his family. He wanted to repopulate his country and ordered every woman to produce five children. I wonder if he ever saw the plight of these little ones, who were in such a terrible state, and were the results of mothers who gave birth yet could not feed their children.

A jar of lollipops

A lot of the children who were in those cots had little straight-jacket restraints and were sat with their arms folded across their chests because out of lack of stimulation they had become self-harming, picking and scratching at their own skin. At this I needed to get out of there because I was absolutely traumatized. The sight and smells were overwhelming, and I was appalled at the terrible conditions that these children were living in. It was beyond belief. What could I do? I couldn't untie the children or take them out of their cot-beds. Many of them were facially deformed and just communicating with gestures and noises. With only one nurse to care for thirty children there was no-one to shout at or blame because they were doing what they were commanded to do. The only thing I could do was to bring in food, medical supplies, bedding, toiletries, toys, clothes etc. When all was delivered, we felt satisfied that we had done something to help but frustrated at what we had seen.

The staff were speechless, they didn't have the words to express their delight that we had come with all this aid. Mr. Alex took a lot of pleasure in emptying the lorries. It meant going up and down lots of steps and stairs. The building had been converted into dormitories from what was probably a stately home. As I write I wonder what had happened to all those children and what kind of lives they have led. At one point Mr. Alex went running down the orphanage steps to get a large jar of lollipops. As he pulled out the first lollipop he was swarmed with children all with their little hands stretched out to receive one and their gaze fixed on the jar. Mr. Alex was overwhelmed. The adults stood around too, hoping to receive a lollipop themselves. As I looked on this scene I could not only see the delight on the children's faces but also on the face of the giver as well. It was a moment in time where joy had come to those who were downcast. We didn't give the gospel by word, but by deed. The love of Christ was shown by meeting the needs of these vulnerable ones, the ones that no-one wanted or really cared about. These traumatized little ones, especially those with straight jacket type bindings to secure their arms across their chests, was such a cruel sight. How I wanted to love them and pick them up for a cuddle. But I wasn't allowed to. We were only visitors and would be leaving within the hour. We said our farewells and drove back to the Hungarian border, shocked by what we had just observed. The images stay with me to this day.

Mr. Alex and I took turns driving back to Budapest. He told us about his adventures in America and Canada. I was warming to him and to Ann and we got on nicely together. Mr. Alex booked us into a little panzio for the night and that evening he took us out to a traditional Hungarian restaurant in Budapest. We were able to experience the city by night, it was stunning and all lit up. It was the first time I had had a real taste of this city, with its bridges over the beautiful river Danube, palaces, castles, sounds and smells. The next day we flew home. Flying to and from Hungary was definitely the way forward.

This was the early church. The lean-to was made of spare wood and old plastic. Many souls were saved and lots of people healed and delivered. Praise Jesus

Chapter 10

Trips to Hungary

On previous trips I had used Eurolines coaches. The journey from Manchester was about thirty-six hours. I would travel with large suitcases of clothes and shoes and on several occasions pushchairs to pass on to mothers with young children. Hardly any of them would have a pushchair but would carry their little ones round in slings. I would travel wearing three skirts, numerous jumpers and a couple of coats. Although it made me hot I did this so I could give the clothing away. It was worth it just to see the faces of the recipients. I would go to whatever lengths I could to help those very poor people.

The coach journeys were very relaxing and interesting. The people I would meet would be young students, au pairs and grandmothers. I did however have one or two distressing journeys. One time I met a young Hungarian girl who was travelling to England to take up the position as an au pair to a family in Essex. They had three children. She would be able to earn enough money to be able to send some home to her mother to help feed the family. She told me that she had taken out a loan to pay for her ticket. When we arrived in Calais we had to leave the coach to go through customs, then board again at the other side. I got on and waited for Eniko to get back on, but she didn't. I felt concerned that something had happened to her.

When the driver started the engine I jumped up out of my seat.

"Wait, wait." I called, explaining that Eniko was missing.

He informed me that he knew of three people from the coach who didn't have the correct documentation and would either continue in a later coach or be sent back to Hungary. A person behind me said it happened quite often especially if there was a problem with a Visa. It doesn't happen these days as Hungary has joined the E.U.

On another occasion I was bringing Pastor Kati and her worship leader Christian Balough to England. There was a group of "lefties" who were part of a neo-Nazi party which hated Roma people, dark faced people and Jewish people of which Christian was all three. This group were dressed in combat suits and drinking strong alcohol. They made rude gestures to Christian and used terrible swear words. It became so bad that I went to complain to the driver. He said that there was nothing he could do about it but if other people were willing we could swop seats. Nobody wanted to so we had to endure all this until we got to London. On arrival we saw a large crowd of similarly dressed people waiting to welcome the neo-Nazi group. They all wore swastikas. It was quite concerning. The receiving group appeared to be English and the coach group were joining them for some sort of rally. Pastor Kati and Christian were quite traumatized by it all and must have thought all English people were like this. Fortunately, they soon found out differently and I brought both Kati and Dani over to England on two other occasions.

There were times when I drove vans over to Hungary and other times when I towed caravans full of aid. Every trip was quite enjoyable and the scenery magnificent. The adventure and meeting people overrode the distance I had to drive. Indeed, my actions are not those of a normal person because truly it is the Holy Spirit prompting me and the word of God that drives, activates and enables me to do all these things. God always told me, you are my daughter, you can do it and you will do it. On the other hand, people would say to me, don't do it, you can't do it. It is still like that to this very day. These mission trips in the early nineties whether I went by coach, drove or flew were very enjoyable, meaningful and with purpose. When you have a purpose you have to have a result. These trips laid the foundations for what God wanted me to do in Hungary. I didn't know how or where it was all heading in those days or even what God was doing but I was now five or six years into my Christian walk and I was learning to trust in the lord with every step of the way.

Kati and Dani's family

On every trip I made I stayed in Nyirbeltek, welcomed into the humble home of Dani and Kati. There I could laugh and be happy as I was accepted by the people for just who I was. I found great love there, not just from Dani and Kati, but from Kati's parents, Zoltan and Elona Balough. Kati's father lived in a much nicer house up on the top road. He was a very well-set man and his skin was very dark. He was Mongolian looking and had the deepest voice I have ever heard. He took me in as his daughter. His wife, Elona, was fair skinned with beautiful blue eyes that shone brightly every time she saw me. She would pinch my cheeks and say,

"en najon seretlek melani." (I love you very much Melanie).

"Te vagy a lanyom," (you are my daughter).

They were a very happy couple in their sixties and had been married over forty years. They had six daughters, Tunde, Elona, Erika, Margot, Peroska and Kati, and one son called Zole. They all had husbands, wife and children and I was accepted and loved by every one of them.

Tunda lived next door but one to her parents. She made the most delicious Shutni, (cake) and would always want to feed me. Erika sold bric-a-brac in the little piazza, where there was a small market. She would always give me shoes or a jumper or a scarf. She was the first one in Hungary to name her baby after me, Melanie. (I now have five children named after me). You could not call your children by a foreign name in Hungary in those days. You had to call them by a name listed for the month of their birth. Hence there are a lot of people with two names such as Pastor Kati (her known name) but whose real name is

Zsuzsanna. The latter name was picked from the list of January, the month she was born.

They have always been a close family, but a rift came between them all when Kati became a Christian, a pastor and an evangelist and as her Christian activities overtook her life. So many foreigners have been wonderfully hosted by Dani and Kati, yet it changed the whole structure of the family in this tiny, sleepy village sitting on the Romanian border.

Dani had never really left the village from his childhood except for the odd occasion when he had to go to Budapest to do some manual work. There was no work in the village then nor even at this present time. Both Dani's and Kati's families lived in the village, so it was a very tight community where everybody is related to someone.

As their church grew in number, I brought in many Christian pastors, preachers, evangelists and prophets from all over the world and it did disturb things. The people I brought in as part of my team came to help build the Christian community in this area. The families had never seen a true black face like the one that came with Arlene from Guadeloupe. Nor had they ever heard American accents, like the ones that came with the prophetess Deborah Sweetin, and Battle Cry Ministries. There were many others from different countries including, Chinese, Indian, Welsh, Scottish and Irish. This disturbed the family because their beloved Kati had other interests now that looked out of the family community. Kati and Dani revelled in it and were perfect hosts. As more grandchildren came into the family, so they became reunited again and love prevailed, which is always the substance that builds the family and makes it secure.

The house

By now I had started to send out small donations to Dani and Kati, ten maybe twenty pounds a month so that they could feed the village children and also as an incentive to teach the children about the bible. It was 1996. Dani had made a plastic lean-to on the outside wall of his house to use as a meeting place for the children. By 1997 not only were the children coming but men and women too. They wanted to learn the bible and so the church was birthed. I had such a love for these people and I would visit them two or three times a year.

It was to be several years later in 2000 when we bought the church house. It was a very sad year for me as my middle son, Johnny, had passed away in the April, aged only twenty-seven. I was distraught with grief. I fled out to Hungary to be comforted by my Hungarian family who loved and cared for me through that traumatic time. One of my church elders, Freda Westwood, came with me. She loved the Lord and was happy to accompany me to do the Lord's work in Hungary. Freda had seen the little plastic lean-to which by now was totally inadequate, battered by the winter snows and the winds of spring, yet it was still overflowing with people.

On one occasion we went to visit Kati and Dani's parents on the top road called Zrinyi ut. It was brought to our attention that the bungalow next door to them was empty and up for sale. The Lord had already laid it on my heart that we should start looking for a new building but in the natural it was beyond me to even think about the cost or how such a venture could be funded. I was still learning to trust the Lord in the small things and He was teaching me to listen to His voice when He spoke. I asked my Christian sister Freda if she would go and pray quietly on her own and ask the Lord whether we should buy this house. We had already looked at its location. It was sandwiched in between Kati's parent's house on the right and her sister's house on the left. Her brother's house was situated to the rear of the property. For security reasons it was sound. The house, or should I say bungalow had four large rooms, a stable attached at the rear and a garden. Freda came back after a while,
"Yes," she said, and I didn't question her because I knew the Lord had answered.

The next thing to do was to find out who owned the bungalow. Dani and Kati were elated at the thoughts of us looking to buy them a home and the idea of using the stable as a church. The people who owned the bungalow were the local policeman and his sister who was a senior staff nurse in the sanatorium in Nyirbeltek. I had actually been there a year before with Mr. Alex and Ann on a previous mission to deliver some blankets. This nurse happened to be the very one who had looked after us and she remembered us. The brother and sister had inherited the house from their mother who had recently passed away.

I think it was the next day when we were able to arrange a meeting with the policeman and his sister. They were asking so many millions of forint and my heart sunk. I hadn't really got to grips with the exchange rate, but it seemed an astronomical amount of money which of course we didn't have. Kati is a wonderful negotiator and was soon bartering in millions on my behalf. I asked her to stop so that I could look at the exchange rate as I knew we simply didn't have that amount of money and we were only making enquiries at this point. By now however, the dealings had continued and I was checking on my calculator to find the pounds equivalent, it was £4,500. That alone shocked me as I was thinking about the cost of housing back home and expecting the cost to be more like £20,000-£30,000 for such a sizeable place.

Well, by now Kati had got the price down even lower to what seemed to be the forint equivalent of about £2,500 and I cannot tell you the excitement in my heart when Kati nodded her head and I said,
"Yes, we shall have it." I shook his hand.
The smiles on his and his sister's faces showed that they were very happy with the agreement, it was a "done deal." We were all shocked but so elated, happy that we had bought the building and still wondering how we were going to pay for it. But the Lord had said yes, so I had to learn to trust Him.

A step of faith

The next day Kati had made an appointment for us to see a solicitor in her office in Nyirbator and we were to meet her that very same day. What a shock, the papers were already drawn up and all we had to do was sign….and pay! We hadn't realized that we were expected to pay the whole amount that very day. Now Mr. Alex had given me £500 in cash to take all the village children to the zoo. I decided that I could use that and then I would only need to raise the other £2,000 and a miracle! The only way I could access that amount of money was from my credit cards. Now I hope you readers will understand what a great financial risk it was to me and that it would be a huge disappointment to Kati and Dani if I didn't get it.

BUT WE PRAYED

I wasn't a pretty sight to look at as I was still dressed in black as is the family custom when in mourning the loss of my son. I trotted off to the bank in Nyirbator to explain my predicament and ask to draw £1,000 each from my credit cards. To mine and everyone else's surprise I came out of the bank with two carrier bags of money. I wasn't sure exactly how many forint there were as the exchange rate was changing all the time. Would you believe it? I walked back to the solicitor's office where they were all waiting for me in anticipation. The paper money was tipped out on the table in front of the solicitor. She counted it out and gave the policeman and his sister half each after her fees had been paid. It was just the right amount of Forint which was the equivalent over £2,000! This had to be a miracle. We were all overjoyed.

I signed the paperwork for the house. The policeman handed me the big, rusty key, shook my hand and left with his sister. I had the documents and deeds put in Dani and Kati's names to show that I wasn't buying it as a personal investment and that I wouldn't sell it from under them. It was theirs, all theirs. Really this was a Godly seed being sown into the lives of this community and into this country. I happily did what the Lord had told me to do. I had no idea how I was going to pay back the money. I laughed to myself as I saw what the Lord had done. I still have the credit card statements to this very day, being twenty years on.

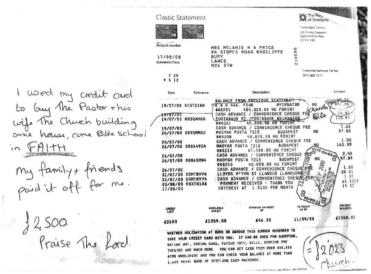

Credit card statement of the purchase of the first mission house.

Dr. Stefán Éva
ügyvéd, adószámadó
4350 Nyírbátor, Kossuth u. 34.
Tel: 06 (42) 284-259
Adószám: 3385411-1-35

Adásvételi szerződés

Készült az alábbi helyen és időben egyrészről Olajos László gyuláné Kiss Margit / an: Kiss Margit szsz: 2 60 ... / Nyírbéltek Kossuth u 24/a., Kiss János / an: Kiss Margit szsz: 1 65 ... / Nyírbéltek Vasvári P u 44.szám alatti lakosok mint eladók, másrészt **Beri Dánielné Balogh Zsuzsanna** / an: Kanalas Ilona szsz: 2 610118 4910 / **Nyírbéltek Jókai u.10.** szám alatti lakos mint vevő között az alábbi feltételek szerint :

1./ Eladók eladják a **nyírbélteki 884. hrsz** alatti 1397 m2 területű **Zrínyi u.3.szám** alatti 2 szoba komfortos házasingatlant **1.000.000 ft vételárért.**

2./ Vevő az 1.pontban írt ingatlant az ottani vételáron megvásárolja. A vételárat a szerződés aláírásakor megfizette az eladók részére, melynek felvételét az eladók a szerződés aláírásával elismerik.

3./ Eladók hozzájárulnak ahhoz,hogy az 1.pontban írt ingatlanra a vevő tulajdonjoga az ingatlannyilvántartásban is bejegyzést nyerjen **vétel jogcímén.**

4./ Vevő az ingatlanok birtokába a **szerződés aláírásakor** léphet, birtokbalépéstől viseli annak terheit és húzza hasznait.

5./ Szerződő felek meghízási adnak **dr. Stefán Éva** ügyvéd részére az okirat elkészítésére és a képviseletükre,aki az okiratot is ellenjegyzi.

6./ Az eljárás költsége és illetéke a **vevő** terhe.

7./ Szerződő felek magyar állampolgárok , nagykorúak.
Ezt a szerződést megértés után mint akaratukkal megegyezőt ügyvéd előtt aláírták.

Nyírbéltek 2000. julius ...

Olajos László Gyuláné adósz: ...

Kiss János adósz:

Béri Dánielné adósz: ...

Előttünk mint tanuk előtt:

Ellenjegyeztem: dr. Stefán Éva ügyvéd

Witnessed this day by. 17.7.2000.
Melanie Price.
and
FREDA WESTWOOD
F Westwood

Dr. Stefán Éva
ügyvéd, adószámadó
4350 Nyírbátor, Kossuth u 34.
Tel: 06 (42) 284-259
Adószám: 3385411-1-35

Receiving the deeds to the house

REVELATION 22.v. 17.   **✝**   PASTOR: DANI, KATI BERI

TEL.: 0036-42-389-091

CHURCH OF THE WATER OF LIFE
NYÍRBÉLTEK, JÓKAI U. 10.
HUNGARY

DEAR Sister Melanie and Julia Rita
Thank you for Letter and gift.
Thank you telefone
you rajt Letter. OK. Melanie
Come, come Nyirbeltek CHURCH VIZIT
wi LAV you Jesus name.
foto grasz cigane.
— Hello.
Melanie PLiz HeLp House vorba
Mr. ALex House Big very very
gut, House one million.
cigane → Piko csavo Dani No House 2 chirden.
Sister HeLp. Jesus name.
Lov Lov
Pastor Dani + Kati cigane
CHURCH. ✂ ✂
☺

The whole joy of doing that was the start of the healing balm of my bereavement. God was doing a work in me.

When I returned home Mr. Alex paid off £1,000 of my credit card bills but not before telling me that I was a Silly Billy! However, he loved anybody who was prepared to take a challenge. Family and friends paid off the rest. I cannot say that I paid for any of it, the Lord provided. All glory goes to Jesus because that is who this work is about.

Let the work begin

Having secured our first property with an acre and a half of land Dani and Katie could now move to their new house. It

124

just needed a good clean and the walls painting. We explained to the children that we couldn't take them to the zoo as we had used the money to buy the church house and asked them to forgive us, which they did.

Children help out

They were only too happy to come along and help with the garden. They plucked up the grass with their bare hands as we had no tools. How joyfully they did it too. In the front garden of the house was a little round well where you lowered a wooden bucket down into the earth to draw water. It was lovely.

Just to add here, the children did go to the zoo, Freda paid for it out of her own money before we left.

Dani and Kati's old house in the poorest part of the village was given to their son, Dani junior, and his wife, Valeria, who had two children. They were very happy because prior to that they had been living with his wife's mother in one room in her tiny house. Dani's mother-in-law was happy for them to leave and Kati's parents and sister were also happy to have their family as neighbours. This one course of action had made many people very happy, including Freda and I.

As I said before there was a horse stable attached to the back of the house, with a door leading into it from the kitchen.

Through the stable to the rear another door led into the garden. In Hungary, as in many other countries, people would keep their livestock such as horses, chickens, ducks, and goats very close to, or even in the house. The stable was about thirty-two feet long and seventeen feet wide with a roof made of straw. Dani, Kati and the villagers soon turned it into a nice little meeting place for the church. They covered the outside of the roof with tin sheets and inside with plasterboard leaving the straw in place for insulation. People began to bring a chair here and a chair there. The church was birthed.

After praying and fasting Dani, Kati and I decided that it should be called "The Church of the Living Waters." Every Sunday it was packed to overflowing. Dani and Kati became both worship leaders and pastors. Kati can sing like a bird and Dani could play the guitar, the accordion and the keyboard. Kati studied the bible for two hours every morning and still does. She would ask the Lord to give her the right word to preach to the people. It was amazing for when she prayed for people they were healed. When she called for people to give their lives to Jesus, the men, women and youth would come weeping, with repentant hearts. The Holy Spirit of the Living God had brought the presence of the Lord to these poor rejected and forgotten people. As the name of Jesus was proclaimed through the villages, the church added to its numbers.

Something amazing was happening in front of our eyes. We could see a transformation in the peoples' faces. It was as if a light had been lit up in them which radiated out to their family and friends in the village. After two years the whole social atmosphere had changed. Men had given up smoking, drinking and beating their wives, women had stopped swearing and cursing, there was unity amongst families, the people had smiles on their faces and The Church of the Living Waters flourished. I can't say it was a revival because revival means it has happened before but here nothing like this had ever happened before. God was doing a new thing, shining a bright light on His people and they got saved, delivered and healed. The school teachers would come down to the village to ask Dani and Kati how come the children were moving up to a higher grade in their reading and writing so quickly. Kati could only say that the children loved reading and writing about the bible stories and they enjoyed it.

A second house

When we realized that the stable church couldn't hold the number of people who were coming and with winter approaching, we prayed for guidance as to whether we should get another building. Outside of church hours Dani and Kati were inundated with people who would come asking for prayer, or to use the phone, or if they had a pain killer tablet or simply to share their family problems. Dani and Kati were exhausted. It wasn't too long before the Lord showed us another place just across the road at the four lane ends junction. It was a sizeable building with about an acre of land and wrought iron fencing around its perimeter. It was quite run-down and the man who lived there was moving to another village with his family. We eventually bought that building in 2003 at a cost of £3,500. I had managed to raise most of the money at home in Bolton by doing charity stalls outside the town hall. It was quite hard work but lots of fun.

So now we had two buildings and each one had to be maintained and of course there were two electricity bills to pay. This new building became the main church house and community centre. It freed up Dani and Kati's house so that they could entertain ministers and speakers who came in from out of town. Kati taught people to cook and gave lessons in hygiene. A lot of the women lacked in personal hygiene, they wore neither bras nor knickers, they didn't have soap, shampoo or sanitary products for themselves nor nappies for the babies. The odours from the church house were definitely not good. This was soon rectified by Kati's teaching and loving support. We soon had nappies and sanitary wear coming in. The young mothers would bring their babies along. All babies were breast-fed, baby bottles and food were a luxury they couldn't enjoy.

She organised a driving instructor to come and teach people driving theory as they learned to drive. The people were not only hungry to learn but also willing to help in practical ways. They didn't have jobs in these remote villages and they gave freely of their labour by painting the buildings, cleaning the two properties and planting vegetables such as carrots, potatoes and onions. Now we had two functional buildings to the Glory of God and were making His presence known in N.E. Hungary. It was from this little village that we later branched out to do an evangelistic outreach. First of all we went into the next village, Pereche, where just one person got saved. Then week by week more people came to hear the preaching of Pastor Kati. After Pereche came Hadju Hataz and Nyirivish Vari and many other villages. We crossed over the borders to Romania, Serbia and Ukraine to set up house churches and to evangelise.

"So shall my word be that goes out of my mouth, it shall not return to me void, but it shall accomplish that which I please and it shall prosper in the thing I sent it to do." (Is.55 v.11)

How true it is when the Lord sends the seed of His word to be planted in other nations and waters it, how big it will grow.

Jesus said,
"The kingdom of heaven is like to a grain of mustard seed which a man took and sowed in his field which indeed is the least of all seeds, but when it is grown it is the greatest among herbs and becomes a tree so that the birds of the air come and lodge in the branches thereof. (Matt.13 v31-32)

It's like the good seed sown into good soil that has brought in a harvest of thousands of saved souls.

Chapter 11

Johnny

In the last chapter I mentioned briefly that I had gone to Hungary to stay with Kati whilst I was mourning my son Johnny's death. In life everybody has heartache and pain and every family will have deaths and sometimes tragedies. None of us know what tomorrow will bring. We can say that sometimes our worst fears come upon us. As mothers our worst fear is to lose one of our children through death or tragic circumstances. My middle son was called Joseph Creddy Price, meaning in Welsh, Joseph the believer. The name Creddy comes from the word credible. As much as I loved all of my children equally, Johnny shone out because he was such an extrovert.

Johnny

He was a larger than life character who loved life and people. He grew to be over six feet tall and weighed about seventeen stones. He was very handsome with his rows of white teeth which flashed when his mouth beamed with a smile. He was noted for this. He had a mop of black curls on his head. When he spoke it was with a very loud voice. He could sing, dance and play the guitar. Everybody loved Johnny both inside and outside of the Roma community, which itself was now evolving into something more secular. It was becoming acceptable for the young men to step out into the wider community.

Johnny became a professional boxer when he was seventeen and was also branching out into acting and singing on stage. He was a Christian with very strong beliefs and he read the bible every day. He was to fight in the ring at Old Trafford on the same billing as Chris Eubank and Nigel Benn. Nigel and Johnny had made a pact that if they didn't win their fights they would give up boxing and serve the Lord. Nigel Benn went twelve gruelling rounds with Chris Eubank but he didn't win. Johnny didn't get to fight because the time had run out. As a result both men went on to serve God. Nigel went out to pastor a church in Majorca and Johnny went on to become an evangelist in Phoenix, Arizona. God had a plan and a purpose and disappointing though it was for both men to give up boxing, Father God had a plan, and a bigger and better calling for them.

Although Johnny was a boxer, he was very much a Christian and he loved to attend the Roma Gypsy Traveller church. He was able to go out on the streets evangelizing with the men of the church. He loved to play his guitar and sing worship songs unto the Lord. He didn't have the most brilliant voice and was often off key but his showmanship and panache in delivering a song made you laugh.

This was reflected in his love for the singer, Al Johnson who was a little Jewish man who loved to make people happy through his songs. He would dress up as a minstrel, blackening his face and perform wearing white gloves. Johnny was awed by this little man and went on to perform like him. He made one of his performances on the T.V. show "Stars in your Eyes," at the Monaco Ballroom in Wigan, to raise money for the Lord Mayors Charity. The performance took place just two days before he died. It was the Wednesday and by Friday night he was dead.

He was on his way to a wedding in Banbury on the Saturday, where he was to be the best man for Michael Riley. Johnny actually died in Middlewich on his Uncle Tom's caravan park on the way to the wedding. He was taking his touring caravan down to Banbury and it was a faulty heater in it that caused Johnny's death from carbon monoxide fumes.

Just three weeks prior to this I had just buried one of my best friends, Lynette Mulenga. She was just thirty-three years old. I was devastated.

Shut up, shut up!

I was emotionally drained. I had lost my best friend and so I went to Anglesey to spend a relaxing weekend with some friends and pull myself together. I invited my friend Rita to come along and we travelled to Llangoed to stay at the Old School with some people from Kidsgrove Methodist church who were there for a few days of fellowship and walking. The Old School was a holiday home for children with special needs and disabilities from the North Staffordshire area, provided by Mr. Alex. Sometimes we used it as a Christian holiday home. It was now Sunday and I had had a wonderful time with this sixty and seventy year old group of people. We walked to Penman Point and the Old Lighthouse at Black Point, where the famous author Enid Blyton had written her children's stories, mentioning these places. It was a glorious day and we had just returned, it would be about two o'clock. I was making tea for us all and the phone rang. Rita picked it up. It was my sister-in-law Betty. Suddenly Rita began hysterically screaming the words ....
"Johnny's dead, Johnny's dead."

I was stunned for a moment by her words as they sunk into my head.

"Shut up, shut up, SHUT UP." I was yelling at her.

No parent should hear these words.

"NO, NO," I screamed and screamed and screamed, it could not be true.

I remember all the guests looking at me in shock. Then my thoughts turned to them, I think I was frightening them as I sobbed uncontrollably. I told them I was sorry but I had to leave and could they lock up when they left.

Rita wanted to drive the two and a half hours journey back to Middlewich but I said no. I thought the driving would keep my mind focused on the road and not on the words Rita had spoken about Johnny. I simply could not believe it. Of course, it wasn't true anyway. My driving wasn't so good and I lost sense of direction and it took nearly three and a half hours to get back. My heart felt like it was cracking open. From time to time my sister-in-law Betty was ringing to see how far away I was. By now the police had been summoned to the caravan park and waiting for an ambulance to take Johnny to the hospital. I yelled down the phone,

"Don't move my son, do not move him. I need to see him there."

I knew that the men in the family had the capacity to stop anyone taking my son away.

When I arrived at the caravan park there were lots of people just standing, not in clusters but individually, with their heads bowed to the ground. I parked my car and even as I walked to the caravan they did not move or look up. They were all traumatized. I approached the little caravan to the sounds of crying and wailing from my two other sons. They were laid over Johnny's body weeping inconsolably. I moved them out of the way so I could look at my son. The reality had not even hit me until then. He was lying in the bed as though sleeping. There was no blood, no smell, no unusual marking on his body. I was stunned and I cried out,

"WHAT'S HAPPENED, WHAT'S HAPPENED?"
I thought maybe someone had killed him. I was told that it was carbon monoxide poisoning from the little caravan heater.

When I looked at my son's beautiful, handsome face still unmoved in the bed, I could see the silent killer of the poisonous gas had turned the left side of his face yellow.

By now it was Sunday and he had been dead thirty-six hours. No-one had missed seeing him on Saturday. My brother-in-law Tom knew that he was going to a wedding on the Saturday. He came back from work on Saturday afternoon and although he noticed Johnny's car outside the caravan didn't think too much of it at that time. Johnny had just bought himself a Mercedes. However when Sunday morning came and no-one had seen Johnny going out for his early two mile run and the car still in the same position, he thought it was quite unusual and went from his house at the top end of the park, down to the little caravan.

Now Uncle Tom was absolutely infatuated with Johnny, he loved him as his own son. He banged on the caravan door. The door was locked and the curtains drawn. Tom had a gut feeling that something was the matter, something was not quite right. He went to fetch a pair of ladders, climbed onto the caravan roof and looked through the skylight. There he saw my Johnny lying motionless in the bed. He nearly fell off the ladders with shock, for he was almost certain that Johnny was dead.

I tried praying over Johnny to raise him from the dead, I believe in it and Jesus told us to do it. Johnny did not move. I began screaming,
"Johnny get up, arise in Jesus name."
The family thought I had gone mad. By now there was an even bigger crowd of people outside, family, neighbours, friends and residents as well as the police. The mortuary attendants were waiting to move Johnny's body to hospital for examination and the post mortem.

"We must take him now," they explained as they had been waiting a while.

It's horrible when you watch people putting your loved one in a black body bag to take them away. That was the moment I knew he was really dead and he wasn't coming back. By this time I could just see his lovely black curls poking out through the drawstring top of the bag. I couldn't let them take him, I had to go too. My sons and daughters took me in their car to Macclesfield hospital. It was all too horrific.

And yet in all this God still had a plan and purpose and His word was not made null and void by Johnny's death. I didn't know it at the time but there were lots of good things that came out of Johnny's passing. God reminded me of a vision he had given me of a field of fearless sunflowers which represented a field of souls that would be a harvest unto the Lord. The Sunflower Trust is a ministry and a charity which evolved from my first ever trip and was dedicated to him.

At that moment in time I only had a sense of great loss, sadness, disappointment and above all grief. It wasn't until years later that I realized how God keeps His promises and His wonders to perform. The bible says,
"I tell you the truth, unless an ear of wheat falls to the ground and dies, it remains only a single seed. But if it dies it produces many seeds." (NIV. John 12v24).

It was the month of April, the month of Johnny's birthday. Both Lynette and my Johnny's passing were reported in the newspaper. Johnny the gentle giant who raised money for charity and whose memory lives in the hearts of all who knew him. Lynette was the mother of three children who became mother to many children in the community. Lynette's children are in my life to this day. When they see me, they see their mother. They have gone on to be fine upstanding people who contribute to the local areas where they live.

Chapter 12

Lynette

I first met Lynette when one Sunday my pastor had asked me to pick her up from the railway station. Meeting Lynette was a wonderful time in my life, she soon became a beloved Christian sister and close friend. My friendship with this beautiful Zambian girl, lasted for many years. She had three children, Samantha, Godfrey and Clarissa. I was considered to be an aunt and family member to them. They were often at my house eating, singing and praying. Lynette and I set up micro businesses together and we sung in a North West community choir along with my sister Rose. Oh, what happy days we had together. We were as poor as church mice but we lived life laughing, working and praying together. I was introduced to a new Zambian culture and society down in London. Relatives and friends would invite us to coming of age parties and special celebrations, where, as guests, we would be served exotic Zambian food. I was taught to dance as a true Zambian and I loved Zairian music. My dear friend had always wanted me to go to Zambia to meet her family. She also wanted to introduce her three children to their relatives but as they were quite young there didn't seem any possibility of them going.

Fulfilling dreams

In January 1999 we spent a fortnight with her children in Zambia. But how did this come about?

One day while I was looking at Teletext, an advert came up showing a return flight from London to Mombasa from £150 per person. This was incredulous, absolutely unbelievable, as it would normally cost £500 or more for a return ticket in those days.

God seems to use me to allow people's dreams to come true, such as my friend Rita, her dream was to visit Elvis Presley's house in Memphis Tennessee, or Peter Turners dream to go to St. Petersburg in Russia and Robyn Peres dream to go to care for African orphans. Each one of these friends fulfilled their dreams through me and I give God the glory. Besides that the Lord has fulfilled so many of my hearts desires such as going to China to see The Great Wall, the Terracotta Army and to follow the footsteps of Hudson Taylor, the great missionary to the Chinese interior. Then of course to visit Jerusalem, not to mention finding my family which was one of my lifetime ambitions and recently putting my stories into print.

Excitedly I rang Lynette and asked her how far Lusaka in Zambia was from Mombassa in Kenya. She asked why so I told her I had seen the cheap tickets from Manchester advertised. She said it wasn't too far. When I told her the cost of the tickets, she was also very excited and like me began to see the possibility of the trip.

"With God all things are possible." (Matt.19v26)

Now I had lovely missionary friends called Rob and Mary Notman who left my house in Bury with five of their nine children to go to Tanzania to start an orphanage and a school. I looked at my map of Africa and could see Dar es Salaam in Tanzania, on the coast. This was where Mary lived in a mission house. I looked at the possibility of either catching a train or a bus from Mombassa in Kenya to Dar es Salaam in Tanzania, and then spend a couple of days there. Then we could catch a coach to Lusaka, Zambia in the interior. To me it looked pretty straight forward and looked possible. Lynette was as much as an adventurer as I was and saw the possibility, except for one problem, she had no money, but we held on to the fact that with God all things are possible.

I could buy the tickets on my credit cards, two adults and two children, as the third and youngest would sit on our knees. Lynette would bring two computers and a printer that would be

136

sold to her brother for £500. He had an internet café within a big hotel in Lusaka. This sale would cover the cost of hers and the children's fare. It was now possible, so I bought the tickets. I am so glad that I walk by faith and not by sight because I would never dream of doing such things in the natural. So happy was the day when Lynette, her three children and I set off on an adventure to Africa which was so exciting and yet dangerous. It was a trip that was preparing us for things to come. Only God knew what the outcome would be.

No turning back!

So it was, with tickets purchased we set off on our adventure. We landed in Mombassa and decided to hire a minibus and driver to take us south down the coast, to Dar es Salaam where we visited the Notmans and stayed for two nights. The next day we booked coach tickets to take us to Lusaka, it was to be an early start at 5.00a.m. I remember when that coach arrived it was a very misty morning and as the mist cleared, it revealed a rugged old bus, not the deluxe air-conditioned coach as was advertised. There was no turning back!! We settled down, the coach was full and all the windows were open as the heat of the day was already rising.

The journey was to take many hours with one official stop for a passport check and bus search in Tunduma on the Tanzanian/Zambian border. For the first ten hours we slept. We were able to buy food from the village vendors who were beautiful local women who stretched their necks up to show baskets of produce balanced on their heads, such as dumplings, samosas, mangos and bananas, along with other produce that I did not recognize . As evening approached the coach was still crossing the dry, arid, flat lands. Every now and then someone would bang on the side of the coach requesting a toilet stop, it was often a quick pee behind a bush! Men to the right and women to the left!

One time when the coach stopped the driver put on the lights which attracted a huge swarm of moths inside. Well, as much as I am a woman of faith and prayer, my senses kicked in and fear came upon me. I wrapped my pashmina around me and pulled the baby close to me. I opened the window and bravely fanned them out. We journeyed on and in the distance I could see amazing bolts of lightning and I was glad it wasn't close to us. Sometimes fear does come upon me but I believe God is strengthening my faith through it. When there is nothing I can do in a situation where danger looms, then all I can do is pray and put our lives in the hands of the Lord.

As I said previously, on this trip we had taken the new computers and printer to sell to Lynette's brother to recoup the cost of the tickets. Lynette asked me to watch the luggage hold in case someone tried to steal it when we stopped. Arriving at Nakonde in Zambia we all had to get out to have passports checked. It was quite scary as these very officious military men bearing guns disappeared with our passports and we weren't allowed back on the coach until all was checked. This took a couple of hours, then just a little further on we stopped again at a humble little lodge where we were to spend the night. We were able to get some food, it was served on wooden plates. I felt quite afraid and anxious, and insisted that I stayed on the coach to keep an eye on the computers. I dozed a little.

The next morning people piled into the coach for an early start and I thanked God that we had got this far and were still alive! A few miles further on it felt like we were going up hill and the road got narrower until it became a dirt track. We were driving through the Uluguru mountains. The driver was a young man in his twenties. He revved the engine and dropped the gears, the noise was incessant. I became concerned that the coach might break down or the driver didn't know what he was doing. I swapped seats with Lynette so I could look out of the window, then wished I hadn't. We were at the top of a mountain, the wheels of the coach precariously on the edge of the track. Down below I could see elephants looking like the size of mice and clouds of dust thrown up by impala and zebra stampeding across the plains. Lynette and her children could see that I was getting irate. We decided to pray. This woke up fear in the other passengers. The driver pushed the engine of the coach to its limits and black smoke plummeted out of the back. People banged on the sides of the coach demanding that he slowed down. The coach meandered to the mountain peak and even the passengers were troubled. Abruptly it stopped in the middle of nowhere. The only sign of life were a few mud huts.

All of a sudden, a lovely lady dressed in a smart blue suit, white blouse, a red and blue cravat around her neck, black high heels and wonderful long, red, painted finger nails, boarded the coach. I sat the baby on my knee and gestured to the lady that there was a seat next to me. With a beautiful smile she said hello and introduced herself as Margaret as she settled into the seat. I was dreading the time when the driver put his foot down again. Relief! I noticed that he had swapped roles with the conductor who was now at the wheel and ready to leave. I shouted across to Lynette,

"Pray Lynette, pray."

The lady called Margaret said,

"Ma'am do not be afraid, I catch this coach every Tuesday. I've been home to my village, but I live and work in Lusaka. These drivers know every pothole in the road. They return on Thursday. They have a schedule to work to and are noted for being on time."

I felt a little calmer and more at ease as we chatted and I was oblivious to the speed of the coach as it came down the mountain.

About three hours later we had arrived in Lusaka. We got off the coach, what a sight we were. Lynette's brother couldn't help laughing at the dishevelled state of us all. One wet and smelly baby, Lynette's dress drowned with wee and she was sweating profusely, three year old Godfrey had found comfort in pulling her hair out and poor little Samantha was just in shock. I felt tired and dirty, but we had arrived. We thanked the Lord that we had made it safely. We had said our goodbyes to Margaret as we got off the coach but looking around the passengers, I couldn't see her anywhere. I really believe she was an angel sent to comfort me, even if she did say she worked in a bank!

Zambia

My dear sister Lynette had always told me that one day she would take me to see the Victoria Falls which are on the southern border of Zambia and Zimbabwe. One side of the bridge is in Zambia and the other in Zimbabwe. It was our plan for this visit. I longed to see those magnificent Falls that our hero, the great pioneer, adventurer and missionary David Livingstone had set his eyes on. I had read in his book on the early missions that he was the one who had discovered this universal wonder. Unfortunately, Lynette's relative, Uncle Michael, had passed away. She had to leave me with her relatives in Lusaka while she went to Ndola with her three children to express her condolences.

The Mwannanshiku family made me very welcome. They allocated me a lovely girl to escort me everywhere. We visited the market which was a humdrum of activity. There was an assortment of pleasant aromas from foods and spices and stinky smells of animals such as goats and chickens. Some people were cooking bits of meat on skewers on little charcoal fires. I noticed pyramid piles of dried caterpillars, various insects, fish and a variety of exotic fruits. There were racks of apparently westernised designer label clothes but on inspection they were made in China, it made me laugh!

I foolishly bought some very lovely wooden carved animals from the cultural village which is where the poor local people can earn a living by carving and selling little animals or on this occasion big animals. I ended up buying a two foot tall, excellently carved, male chimpanzee with his hand on his son, a hippopotamus and a three foot tall wooden giraffe. There were also coconut shells made into monkeys. I bought about eight pieces and stupidly started bartering to get the price down but then I had a check in my spirit about why I was bartering. I should give him the full price because this was his livelihood, so to his amazement I gave him the full price and he was a very happy man. I didn't think any more of it until later on when I got them home and weird things started happening. With pride, I placed the chimpanzee in my living room on the right-hand side of my fireplace, opposite the stairwell. Every time I went upstairs his eyes would gaze at me and follow me up the stairs. The giraffe was big, so I put it in the cupboard under the stairs. Within days it was covered with a green fungal moss. I told my Christian friends about it and they reminded me of the Ten Commandments not to have any hand-created image of man or animal as they carry a spirit of witchcraft that is crafted into them as they are being made. I really should have known better knowing from the background I had already come from, of fortune telling and spiritual endearment. I had to repent before God and immediately gathered them all up and took them to the incinerator at the waste management centre in Bolton. When Lynette died and my son died within weeks of each other, the following year, my African friends thought it was because we had brought the artefacts back.

I was invited to a wedding of the Strawberry family. On the day, it was lovely to see all the families dressed in wonderful African outfits, made from white material and patterned with large red strawberries. It was a fine wedding where everybody danced and the drums were pounding. Many people asked me to dance but I declined to begin with. They wanted to see the mzungo (white woman) dance. I sat watching the men and women dance but I was really playing it cool. Why, because Lynette had already taught me not only how to dance Zambian style but also the etiquette of when to dance and what moves to make. The drummers would drum for about thirty minutes, then stop and have a drink. Then they would wait for someone to give them more money to continue playing.

So, the next time the music stopped I pulled out my Kwacha (Zambian money) and gave it to the drummers to play. I then started to perform my Zambian dance, slowly, slowly with little moves, a little stamping of the feet, knees apart, tiny little moves of the hips, hands held out to the front as though holding something, neck stretched up and head held high. They tied a chitenge (shawl) around my hips to accentuate the moves. I wasn't allowed to look any man or woman in the eye but had to concentrate on the beat of the music. Then suddenly at the right moment make the movements more dramatic, dropping down low with bent knees, (I couldn't do that now!) almost crouching down, then rising back up to the slower, gentle, rhythmic beat of the drums. At that the people howled, whistled and made wonderfully appreciative noises that this mzungo could dance and they loved me for it. I had now become a true Zambian and they gave me an alcoholic drink to seal it. To African people entertaining and offering food and drink is so important because it is a way of honouring guests. So now Lynette's family and the Lusakan people had taken me into their heart because I was one little woman on my own who was courageous enough to get up and dance with them.

Lynette didn't come back from her Ndola trip for about five days. She was a very well-respected member of her family and Uncle Michael had been like a father to her. She told me that she had to go up to the communal hut to receive her inheritance. All the elders sat in this large hut. Traditionally the wife of the deceased comes out to the hut with a bowl of water and the one to whom she offers it is the one who will take over the deceased's affairs. It was very unusual and concerning to Lynette, that Aunty Dorothy (Uncle Michael's wife), at his request had brought the bowl of water to her. Uncle Michael had two sons who worked in the family transport business so the bowl should really have gone to one of them. She said that she didn't know how to deal with it because it was a big insult to Uncle Michael's sons. Anyway she couldn't stay as she was required back home in Bolton to run our kid's club.

I couldn't bear the thoughts of us all suffering that awful journey back from Lusaka to Dar es Salaam, so I got out my credit card once again and purchased the four plane tickets from Lusaka back into Kenya. We had had an unforgettable and wonderful trip to Zambia, and I was known in Lusaka as "the white woman who danced." Little did I know that all this was preparation for a mission trip back into Zambia a few year later.

Our Father God knows everything and the following year on March 23rd 2000, Lynette Mulunga died suddenly of an embolism. This completely broke me because I loved her dearly and she left me to be guardian to her three children. She didn't know that she was going to die but would always tell me, the pastor and the family that if anything was to happen to her that I should have the children. Lynette had been separated from her husband and had made a new life for herself in Bolton. I went to comfort her beautiful children. It took eleven days of arrangements for the funeral and sleepless nights of unbelief and devastation before the preparations were completed.

No-one can ever know the impact that Lynette had on my life, especially her beautiful solo singing to the Lord and in the gospel choir. We often drove to London through the night to meet with her African family. I thank the Lord that it was so precious to have a friend of such high calibre. The fact was that she was a friend in a proper and loving way.

We buried Lynette in Bolton next to another Zambian man Mr. Lawrence Chabu after a wonderful funeral service which was a great tribute to her. The singing was led by the North West Gospel Choir. She was dressed in a hand-made wedding dress sewed by Aunty Alice, who was the widow of the High Commissioner in Malawi, and was laid in an open coffin. Her girls had lovely dresses made from the same material and her son looked very smart in his suit. I had everything videoed and sent the film of the whole funeral to her family in Zambia so that they could see that her life was celebrated with honour, for she was a wonderful Christian woman whom I will never forget. Just to add that Mr. Lawrence Chabu, his wife Rachel and children, were wonderful friends who opened their hearts and home to everyone. The door was always open and the smell of food cooking was intoxicating. The combination of a wonderful welcome and hospitality showed how they let the world come in and have a taste of Africa.

Lynette was gone. Now, I was never going to see the Victoria Falls with her.

Lynette left a legacy. We had set up a kid's after school club in Little Lever, Bolton. After she had passed away, I handed the whole business over to the manageress Kath Dunning who was also a Christian. She later developed the club to such a high standard that it was awarded the best after school club in England. The award was presented by Cherie Blair, the then Prime Minister's wife. Lynette lives on in the hearts of the mothers and children who loved this African child carer.

Lynette

Loss

The loss of these two people, my son Johnny and my dear friend Lynette, with just three weeks between them was devastating. I couldn't live without them. With my son, it was about loving him so much and being proud of his achievements. With Lynette it was the loss of special friend who brought laughter and intelligent conversations, and shared our mutual care of the needy, lost and lonely. But, God is always honing us and it hurts. We are sometimes thrown into the fire so that we can be purified like gold. Sometimes God takes away the scaffolding in our lives so that we can totally depend on Him. In losing these two precious people I realize the value of a life and that every single human being is to be valued and cherished. We should live our lives as if today is the last day. That way we not only appreciate other people but value our own lives as well.

From this point in time my life changed dramatically. The fuel for change was in reading my bible, listening to God and understanding that God's calling on my life was more serious than I thought. If I was to benefit any other human being, I had to get out of my black mourning clothes and start living life for Jesus once again. I found comfort in and loved the 'soaking' experience of listening to spiritual worship songs.

As I was still working on the mission fields of Eastern Europe, I gradually realized that there were hundreds of thousands of people who were in similar circumstances to me. However, they had no God in their life, no belief, no faith and no anchor to pull them out of the mire of their grief. But I had Jesus. He always guided me towards the light and enlightenment.

I was still growing as a Christian and doing ministry. I told Father God that as long as he allows me to live, I would serve Him, and Him alone. I would serve people by giving them the Good News of the gospel of Jesus Christ. It was by practising and doing ministry that I got stronger and the heaviness and darkness was blown away by the beautiful Holy Spirit that comforted me, revealed things to me, so kindly counselled me and enabled me to move on and continue serving the nations.

Chapter 13

Sunflower Vision

As I mentioned in the chapter about Johnny, the Lord gave me a vision of a sunflower field and the interpretation was about him. Johnny lived a remarkable life and the Sunflower Trust is dedicated to him.

The sunflower seed is like a flat bean. When it is sown into the ground in March or April, it grows quickly and by July or August it is a fully grown flower reaching heights of up to eight feet. The stem of the flower is bright green and very thick, the flower head is brown and surrounded by golden yellow petals which can turn towards the sun. Its petals stretch out to lap up every ray of heat that the sun has to give. The flower is watered profusely by the spring rains and draws nourishment from its deeply embedded roots. By summer the flower is strong enough to withstand the fierce heat from the sun but the petals distribute the heat evenly on the flower head. Because of the design of the petals the heart of the flower head is rich and full of nectar, sustaining the many insects and creatures which feed on it.

When the flower begins to die it scatters its seeds far and wide. Death is not the end for the sunflower for when it is harvested it has many wonderful uses, aroma therapy oil, beauty purposes for skin and hair, herbal medicine and for cooking (it is used in margarine). The stem is used for silage and fodder.

The interpretation of the vision is about Johnny's life. He was just a simple little gypsy boy who was planted into the Christian faith and chosen by the Lord for a purpose. He grew very quickly in stature and strength, his beauty was radiated by his aura, which was the light of the Lord shining through him. As he grew in years his head was turned to the sun, that is, the Son of God, Jesus Christ. His seeds were the words of truth, the words of life, the living word of God, the gospel, which was sown into the lives of other people. His oil was the anointed oil of the Holy Spirit that lived in him and spurred him on to do the things the Lord wanted him to do and go where he was led. His faith and beliefs were his roots that came from his fervent teachings from the bible and were rooted deep into his mind and soul. They were written on his heart and came forth from his mouth. Johnny lapped up the warm love that ever surrounded and enveloped him. That was the agape love of God as He caused His face to shine upon him. Johnny radiated love to all who encountered him just like the petals of the sunflower. His seeds have been spread far and wide as he told people about the love of God and encouraged those who gave their lives to the Lord.

Johnny died on 15th April 2000 aged just twenty-seven years. He lives on in the lives of the people he brought love to.

The Sunflower Trust

The Sunflower Trust is a ministry and charity supporting children in Nyirbeltek, Hungary. The vision applies to these children too, as they are sown into the church and bible school which we planted and equipped there in 1996. Their faces are turning to the Son, Jesus, and they feel the love and the spark of hope for a better future and knowledge of worth. They are being equipped to go forth into the world to bring the Good News.

The Sunflower Trust was started in 1989 when I, as a young Christian, was serving the Lord by taking aid to Eastern Europe, primarily to Romania. Year by year I would go out to both Romania and Hungary and see the poverty and hunger there, and the need to help people who were trying to help themselves. I opened a bank account in 2003 and set the charity with four trustees and called it The Sunflower Trust. It was mainly called a trust because from the beginning we prayed that we would always be volunteers and we would not take any money out of this charitable account for our personal expenses.

This was the principal of George Muller who said that he would only ask God to meet their financial needs and bring in their provisions.

We could not ask anybody for help or fundraise, so that way it kept everything clean with no corruption. The money that goes into The Sunflower Trust was and is from a handful of close friends and family. Unlike any other charitable cause, every penny goes straight out to the needy and nothing comes out for expenses or overheads. God is so wise because those people who travel with me are required to pay for their own flights and expenses and that shows their heart of sacrifice and giving to achieve God's purposes.

This work is a holy, clean work and it is a kingdom building work as soul after soul are saved, when little prayer groups become fellowships, churches are planted, communities are changed, people's mind-sets are broken, lives are renewed, people are healed, delivered and made whole again, all done with all authority in Jesus name. It is the same today and the constitution has never changed. The love of Jesus for the people is the centre.

For further information and historical record of the charity and the ministry go to Facebook The Sunflower Trust or our website, www.thesunflowertrust.org.uk

The Falconer Children's Home
Zambia

Chapter 14

Mama Lilias Falconer

However, it was just a year and a half later that I was asked by an elder of the church if I would like to go to Zambia to assess an orphanage which a group of elderly women, in the Christian community, had been supporting for over fifty years. All my expenses would be met by these ladies. I was surprised and honoured to be asked, but I was just the person for the job as I was akin to Zambia and the Zambian people.

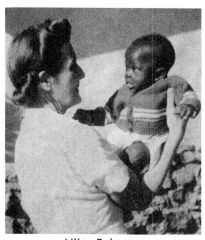

Lilias Falconer

I was to visit The Falconer Children's Home, an orphanage, which had been set up by Lilias Falconer who was born in Manchester in 1915. At the age of fifteen she had told her family that she wanted to go to Africa, "to look after babies and children." In 1939 she was trained as a nurse by the Salvation Army. She then took a course in tropical medicine. Lilias sailed for Africa where she saw the plight of babies left to die after their mothers had died in childbirth. She agreed to look after one such child, but soon five more were brought to her. Lilias went further out into the bush where, in 1947, she established her Children's Home and Orphanage in the small village of Kabulamema. No child was ever refused admission. In 1969 Miss Falconer was included in the president Kenneth Kaunda's honours list. (www.Falconertrust).

Mama Lilias was awarded an M.B.E for welfare services to thousands of Zambian children. She would not leave the babies to come back to England to receive it. "Mama" as she was called died in 1998. Her wish was that her work be carried on by her children. Her success story of the Home is that some of the children stayed and were trained, willing, able and ready to continue the running of the home. Simon Samutala became the general administrator. He originally came to the home as a two day old baby. (www.thefalconertrust.org) The welcome sign in front of the home reads,
"Who so shall receive one such little child in My name receives, Me."

The flight

After learning about Mama Lilias Falconer and meeting up with the last of her very elderly supporters I had a better understanding of where we were going and what we were going for.

On the fifth of August 2003 Freda Westward and I boarded the plane for Lusaka, it was an overnight flight. We arrived about six fifteen in the early morning and after collecting our luggage we took a taxi to The Reed Mat Lodge at Kaunda Square. It was about fifteen minutes' drive from the airport. We were pleasantly surprised at this Christian lodge. I had only found and booked it a few nights before we left. It was the cheapest I could find and was nearest to the city centre. We had our own girl, Bonny, to look after us. The first day we arrived I felt a little fatigued and nauseated but after a good morning's sleep I felt much better. We spent most of the day lounging around in the grounds of the lodge. That night, after an evening meal of pork loin, mashed potatoes and home-grown salad, we slept like logs.

The next day was the fifth day of the seventy-seventh Zambian agricultural show. People were arriving from all parts of Africa to visit this great show. We hopped on a little bus to get to the showground. It was a wonderful experience. Then the following day we flew to Kabulamema.

Freda Westward and I took a Christian Aviation plane, a six-seater Cessna, from Lusaka to the Kabulamema area. My heart almost failed when I saw the small aircraft which was just about as big as the vehicle I drove at home. Before we boarded it, the pilot leaned on the wing and the aircraft tipped to one side.

Mission Aviation Fellowship, Kabulamema

Were we really going to fly a thousand miles across Zambia in this aircraft? My heart fluttered and fear and anxiety set in. Freda on the other hand was very matter of fact and just climbed in and settled in her seat with great composure. As for me, the well-travelled missionary, I nearly fainted just getting on the

153

plane! There were two other passengers who were to be dropped off en route. I have to admit that I was very afraid, but after a short bumpy run down the runway, I couldn't believe how quickly we were in the air. I hesitantly looked out of the window. The views were amazing. Most of this part of Zambia comprises of hills and bushland. The bush is so big and thick that you cannot see the multitude of little villages that are hidden in there. The plane landed at two mission stations where a young missionary left us at one and then a young doctor took his leave at the next. The plane took off and we were up in the air again, the next stop would be Kabulamema on the borders of the Congo. Anxious to get there I peered out of the tiny windows and before long I spotted a vehicle with four or five men in it. They were looking up at the plane and all held guns pointing towards us. For a moment I thought to myself, oh my goodness, we shouldn't have done it this way!

As we got nearer to the ground I could see that the men were waving their arms in the air excitedly. I felt more peaceful and my own excitement replaced the fear. That was definitely from the Lord. We actually landed on a small airstrip which had been created within the bush and the plane came to a stop. The people knew we were coming that week, but they didn't know on which day. The men approached, singing and rejoicing as is their way. After introducing himself to us, a man called Simon Samutala, introduced the other men to us. What a warm welcome we received.

We climbed into the four by four vehicle and Simon, who we now understood to be the manager and supervisor of the Falconer Children's Home began to explain to us that his friend, the bank manager in Lusaka, had sent the loan of the vehicle especially for our visit. He had kindly provided a driver, who was more excited than the others to see us. We set off but as he drove, the driver seemed to be looking in his mirror at Freda and I and looking less at the road. He had a big smile on his face.

Suddenly the vehicle veered out of the bush onto what I can only describe as a wide, brown, river of dried mud. We turned right onto it and continued on a thirty-kilometre journey. Although it was August it was the winter season there, but fortunately there had been very little rain and the heat was intense, so the river was dry. We were the only vehicle on this vast expanse of mud. Eventually we turned sharply left onto a narrow dirt track which led back into the bush. With hindsight I could see that he was taking a short-cut, but after about ten minutes of driving he stopped the vehicle and pulled a gun out from behind the seat. None of us, including the other men knew what he was going to do. He pointed the gun up into the sky and shot a bird. All I saw were beautiful, colourful feathers floating down. It could have been an exotic parrot or a bird of paradise. I don't know, it happened so quickly, then the driver looked at us and laughed. He appeared to be very proud of himself but I, of course, was absolutely disgusted. I made it known that I was very upset that he had killed such a beautiful creature just because he wanted to show off to his passengers. However, I found out later that he was a guide for the game hunters. I would expect him to preserve life, not shoot it!

He got back in the driving seat and in his excitement drove even more erratically than before as the track became narrower. The vehicle swayed from side to side, and at one point a black boar ran right in front of the car. He braked hard and we all screamed. Finally, the dirt track opened up onto a wider track which led us to an opening in the bush. There was a big sign, The Falconer Children's Home and Orphanage.

The Falconer Children's Home

Having arrived, I felt a great sigh of relief, joy and excitement. Once your feet are on terra firma you feel much better and after such a journey we had made it. We pulled up at a single storey building. There was a large group of people in two lines waiting to welcome us. We were the "dignitaries" who had come to visit the outpost! We were introduced to the manageress who was called Miriam and Mama Robina, who was one of the assistants. As we moved along the lines we were introduced, one by one, to everyone who worked there. As we warmly greeted with them all they either curtsied or shook hands. I felt humbled.

On entering the East side of the building there was a lot of activity going on. Miriam led the way. She was one of the first orphans from twenty-nine years ago and thanks to Mama Lilias is now a fully trained nurse and midwife. She works and serves the orphanage and the children by supervising the daily running of the home (which is her home too). She helps to look after the new babies alongside her helpers from the village. I was over awed when I saw all the big black eyes looking up at me. The faces of the babies and toddlers, who were slung on the mama workers backs, were beaming up at Freda and I. Their broad smiles not only showed warmth and a welcome but also great expectation. They stared at us for a while and just looked on in amazement. Every little face waited for our gaze to fall on them and when it did, they would look down in complete and utter shyness. My heart went bump and with a lump in my throat we continued on into the building.

We were shown to our sleeping quarters, at least we had beds with mosquito nets, which was a blessing. We were staying here for a week. The building itself resembled a long, low barracks. It had a long hallway with rooms going off to the left and the right. First impressions were that it smelled quite clean, but the door frames and doors showed that it was quite archaic really. I couldn't hear any young children in this building, but I was aware of some older ones who were playing football outside.

Simon took us into another building, more like an English house, where we were provided with an evening meal. Simon Samutala was one of Mama Lilias's first orphans and so he was regarded as her son. He spoke perfect queen's English, as I am sure Mama Lilias did, but with a Northern accent. His manners were impeccable. He was the "Poirot" of the N.W. borders of Zambia! We sat at a humble table to eat our meal of chicken (which I add was very tough!), with a gravy-like sauce, and "Fufu" and what they called spinach. It was not spinach at all but the green leaf of a root vegetable.

Later on in the same week Freda and I found ourselves at that very same table, eating the same meal, because they cooked the same meal every day, when a youth came in, bowed his knee and gave Simon a letter or document. When Simon looked at it, I was astounded when he announced,

"It's a letter for Mrs. Melanie Price."

I looked at the large envelope I saw that it was a large sheet of paper made into an envelope shape. I opened it, and before I had read a few words, tears welled up in my eyes. The letter was from my eldest daughter who had taken the time and effort to send me a letter telling me that she missed me so much, to look after myself and that she would be praying for me every day until I got home safely to her and the family. The tears rolled down my face until both Freda and Simon began thinking that I had received bad news. Later they realized that they were tears of joy. I have that letter to this very day.

But,......here we are back on the first night of our trip. Freda and I were trying to sleep under our mosquito nets. We were dripping with sweat and our clothes were sticking to us. There was no bathroom or running water in this building. I utilized a little paper waste bin that was in the room as a bucket and filled it with water so we could wash ourselves down with a flannel. Freda wasn't too happy but as I told her,

"This is a mission my dear and this is Africa."

That first night we slept out of sheer exhaustion and woke early to the sounds of cockerels crowing, babies crying and people shuffling about. Our hosts took us back to the house for a breakfast of bread and jam, bananas and milk, served by the housemaid.

Down to the river

Simon took us to Mama Lilias's grave which was situated between the orphanage and the private house where we ate our meals. They really loved their Mama. Now, in the light of day, I could see that we were on a high plateau overlooking the Kobompo river. The river is one of the main tributaries of the Zambesi. It flows entirely in Zambia, rising to the east of the source of the Zambesi in the N.W. province, along the watershed between the Zambesi and the Democratic Republic of Congo river basins (Wikipedia).

Mama Lilias Falconer is buried in a very strategic place overlooking the point where the river bends. They have cemented over her grave and placed a seat which has become a place of repose where you can take in the views of the river and the trees.

The river hosts hippopotamus, crocodiles and a variety of other creatures and you can watch the indigenous peoples in their canoes ferrying goods up and down. We lingered a while, as it was an emotional time and said a prayer for Mama Lilias and the work she had established.

Kobompo river

Then we left that place to get to the "nitty gritty" of what we were there for. We were shown round the nursery area of the home and introduced to the nursery nurses who looked after the few very small babies. At that moment in time there were only about five little ones.

Mama's Robina and Agnes with the new-borns ...

We met Mama Robina again and Mama Agnes. She showed us how they strap the babies to their backs with a cloth sling in traditional African style. Then they would go about their daily tasks, sweeping the nursery floor with a straw brush; washing the feeding utensils and nappies both of which were done in the Kobompo river. I was keen to join them. Freda stayed in the home. I went with Mama Robina down the path to the river and was amazed to see how many people had congregated there. They were all very industrious. Ladies were doing their washing at the water's edge, young boys were splashing around and playing. Other women were fetching their water up in large jars which they balanced on their heads.

Mama Robina told me terrible stories which happened long ago. Some mothers from the village had gone to the river to do their washing. As usual they had put their babies down on the ground. A crocodile had sneaked up and eaten them. So for that reason the nursery nurses were very vigilant and would always have someone watching out. Another story was told about some men in a canoe. They were bringing their goods across from the Congo. They disturbed a group of hippopotamus who then became angry and tipped the canoe over. The men drowned.

I would have loved to dip my toes in the river but I kept well away from the water's edge. One thing that surprised me was that there were not as many mosquitoes as I had expected. I had come armed with every imaginable mosquito repellent that I could find! I had heard of so many cases of malaria including some fatalities and I wasn't taking any risks. When we came back up from the river I was delighted so see the children playing football. They did not have a football but, just like the children I had seen in Romania, they had made a ball from rags tied together and wound around until they had a ball. Their laughter expressed their happiness at this simple game.

Being helpful?

I asked one of the mamas if I could try carrying a baby on my back. It was a bit of a challenge, but it wasn't uncommon to me as I used to carry my own babies in a sling, but to the front.

After some bending and bowing, the mamas managed to tie the baby on my back. They must have chosen the lightest baby as I did not feel any weight. I felt happy and useful and asked what I could do to help with my baby on my back. I wanted to do something practical and helpful. They emphatically said, "No, no Mama Melon." (that's what they called me).

It was because I was a visitor, the dignitary and it was not expected. But, I was very determined to be useful, so after carrying the baby round for a little while I made my decision.

I started in the kitchen which was very old I can tell you. There was no running water, nor even a sink, just large bowls. They did have big containers of fresh water which was drawn from a well, not the river. First of all I filled a bowl of water. Fortunately by now, I had put the baby in a cot. The mamas and children followed me everywhere I went, laughing, giggling and speaking in their own language. I decided the first thing I would do was to clean the cupboards and shelves. I climbed up on a box and with cloth in hand took one swipe from right to left, only to create a downpouring of cockroaches and other creatures that fell all over my head and down my back. I squealed and squealed and squealed, much to the amusement of the onlookers. The mamas and children laughed and laughed at the sight of Mama Melon jumping up and down and writhing about trying to get the creatures off herself. I hate cockroaches but in that country they are just a fact of life and no-one bothers with them.

Quickly I decided that kitchen work was not for me. I moved on to watch the children eating their food. Some fifteen to twenty toddlers sat at little plastic tables just eating the fufu.

161

Meal time for the orphan children

I asked where it came from and how was it cooked? Was I in for a shock! First of all they told me that it was some kind of root, like Cassava. There was so much poison in it that it had to be soaked in the river for many hours before it could be cooked. When I asked where it was cooked, they took me to a single bricked room to one side and situated on its own. Inside there was a large cauldron on top of a fire. Three men with a wooden paddle spoon, taller than any one of them, had to keep stirring it so that it would not stick. This was the daily diet of both the children and the mamas. Sometimes they had fish because they had their own fish pool containing a variety of fish, but mainly Tilapia. They would often have bananas which arrived on a big truck, maybe from a local plantation.

Mama Robina, one of the resident staff and also a former orphan herself, told me another true story about a huge snake that had sneaked its way into the garden near the turkey pens. Now these turkeys were all white and very unusual. They had

162

been given to the children's home to teach the children how to raise fowl. The snake had swallowed a whole turkey and the children were beside themselves because they were in charge of the turkeys. Mama Robina said that all the staff came running when they heard the children crying. They beat the snake on the head with stones, sticks and shovels until it was dead. They then cut the snake open and took the fully feathered turkey out which by this time was dead. They cut the snake up and distributed it amongst the local villagers to cook and have a feast. It is not unusual for locals to eat snakes, rats and mice. Meanwhile the turkey was duly plucked, gutted and roasted for the children and the workers in the Falconer Children's Home.

The Falconer's white turkeys

Freda was with me all the time and was one of the ladies who had supported this orphanage for many, many years. She was in contact with Miriam, who like Simon, had been one of the babies that Mama Lilias had taken in. Now she had been educated and had gained a nursing qualification. She was the second in command and deputy to Simon. She had been to England on two or three occasions and given a report to Freda

163

and the ladies on the annual progress of the Children's home. She explained that it was on her heart for the young girls and boys to learn a trade. Some would go to the college in Lusaka and others would become apprentices to local craftsmen.

At Kabulamema

The whole point of this Children's Home was not just to take in babies and bring them up in an institution but to ensure that every child was valued, taught of the Lord and raised up on the word of God. This, I believe, is how for all these years and for all these children, it has successfully continued. They attend a church in the local village where Pastor Albert, who was also one of the orphans, cares for his congregation with great love and zeal. He himself has a wife and seven children. This faithful, beloved man who teaches about Jesus to his flock had to be lifted by two men onto a rock so he could preach, because he had no legs. I have been so humbled on these trips and by the things I have seen and how having no legs did not break the spirit of this man who preached with Holy Spirit fire and acted with love and compassion for others.

Most of these older people who themselves had come from the orphanage received a small allowance from the home as retired workers. Another man called Francis, was the choirmaster. Oh, how those people could sing to the Lord.

Francis must have been 6'3" tall and very slim. Like all conductors his arms would be thrashing the air to the rhythms of the songs as the people responded.

On this journey I had taken five beautiful shirts which had belonged to my son Johnny and a few other items including a pair of sunglasses. I gave the sunglasses to Francis, they were given and received with great delight. Pastor Albert received a shirt with a shout of joy. The other shirts were for the least fortunate men to have. One man who received a shirt told me that his wife was having a baby and if she had a girl he was going to call her Melanie, after me. And he did.

Mission Accomplished

Freda and I had spent a week there and concluded that it was a well-run and organised home. Simon's next projects were to build a small runway for the planes that came in and out and to prepare a patch of land ready to plant some maize.

So the day came when we were to leave. We got up at five in the morning and everyone in the village turned out to say their farewells. It was one of the most moving moments of my life. During the week we had taught English and English history, we had given a word, and shared our testimonies with Pastor Albert. We had eaten with the big and little children, shared the chores and I had carried babies around on my back. We had held a women's meeting to hear about their lives and to share Jesus. We had listened to the workers and heard about the needs of the home itself and we had danced with the people of Kabulamema. I grew to love them so much in such a short time but I hadn't realized how much, until I was leaving. All the workers and the children congregated in front of the home to say goodbye to us. There were over a hundred of them.

Even the headmaster from the secondary school came out this early in the morning, when the cockerels were still crowing and the steam was rising from the Kobompo river, creating a mist across the land. I could see him standing with his head bowed as indeed was everyone else. He wore a mac which was too short for him and a pair of wellies. It was funny because he did not appear to be wearing anything underneath his mac. Mama Robina was there with her team, some with babies on their backs. Simon Samutala made a wonderful speech of thanks and invited us to come back as soon as God would allow it.

Freda just stood there, she didn't say a word. She was as overwhelmed as I was. All of a sudden a traditional African holler filled the air and the ladies began to dance, it was a farewell dance and everyone was crying, even Simon. That moment in time was so precious not because of their gratitude but because of the bond of love that had been experienced by us all. Physically we couldn't really wait to leave because the conditions were so raw but emotionally we had bonded by the Spirit and with deep love in this Christian children's home in the outback of Zambia.

My emotions were getting the better of me and I was crying and Freda was near to tears. Robert came with the jeep to transport us to the airfield. The children chased after the vehicle as we drove away and the ladies were still dancing and singing blessings over us. The children ran and ran behind us for maybe half a mile or so. Now in the jeep we were able to compose ourselves and take a deep breath before thinking about the flight back in that little Cessna. The plane landed on the cabbage patch runway precisely on time and flew us back to Lusaka.

One would say that this was the end of our mission and it was accomplished to the hilt. As Freda and I gave sighs of relief, we were then looking forward to going to a town called Kitwe which is north of Lusaka, where we would be hosted and looked after by Dr. Joseph Mwila and his wife Lillian.

Joseph and Lillian had been living and studying in Manchester in their younger years. Joseph had studied for a doctorate and Lillian a solicitor. They would come to minister and preach to our church, Kings Church in Little Lever, Bolton.

They were great friends of my Pastors Graham and Jessica Kell. Just when Joseph had gained his PhD the Lord spoke to him and told him to go back to his own country, Zambia, and to plant a church and to set up a children's home. He had no idea how he and his wife could do that as they did not have the funds.

Our church pastors and elders met together and prayed, caught the vision and raised the funds to enable Joseph and Lillian to return to Zambia. They started by evangelising with a view to saving souls, setting up prayer meetings and ultimately a house church. Then they were able to establish a church. All this happened very quickly thanks to God and the men of God who united together with one cause, one aim, and one vision. It came to pass that the church grew very rapidly. When I arrived in Zambia the congregation had grown to over five hundred strong.

My pastor asked if we would pop in and say hello to them. That was all was all we had to do.

But God had other plans.

Victoria falls – 'a dream come true'

Chapter 15

Catapulted into Ministry

I already knew the Mwila's as ministers to our church, but I had not really spoken to them in any depth or built a relationship with them. By this time they had set up Kitwe Street Kids Home and they were both fully fledged pastors. They wanted us to share an evening meal with them on the first night we arrived there. There's something special about sitting around the table and eating together while sharing one's own experiences in life. On this occasion Pastor Joseph asked me to share a little about my life and Christian walk.

After giving a brief account of my life story, my Christian life just amounted to going to church, bible studies and my trip to Zambia with Lynette Mulenga. How small the world is because Joseph knew Lynette's Uncle Michael who ran the transport company in the next town of Ndola. He also knew her father who was a high court judge in Lusaka. All these things set off a nice friendship. Little did I know what God was setting me up for. Lillian asked Freda and I if we would give our testimonies at the women's meeting the following day.

Neither Freda nor I wanted to because we had not come here for that. We looked very bemused if not horrified at the request but Pastor Lillian went on to say that if God had brought us across the miles, all the way to Kitwe, Zambia, then He would have given us something to say. This is typical African mentality, that if God sent you, then you have something to give. We got the message! We gave in reluctantly.

Then I thought to myself, I have given my testimony lots of times at home so this won't be any different will it? Lillian told us there would be twenty to thirty business women attending. That was interesting as I had twenty-eight long, thin, silky scarves in my suitcase which I had brought to give to church women in Kitwe as a gift from England.

The following evening we met up in a one roomed hall and instead of seeing lots of poor, emaciated women, I saw buxom ladies dressed in traditional African outfits. Some had their babies on their backs. We praised and worshipped corporately. It was heavenly. Then Freda gave her five minutes testimony. It was time for me to give my testimony. The women responded by making sounds and pulling faces. Some of them looked sad when I told them that I was orphaned and then taken in marriage, at fourteen years old, to a man who eventually became an alcoholic. I told them that my son died at age twenty-seven, that I had been poor most of my life and the only joy I had in life was in Jesus Christ and the family of God.

The women re-acted so much that pastor Lillian had to calm them down and ask me to conclude. I did so by saying that no matter what I had suffered in life, my life in Jesus had brought me great joy and happiness. I had found my family in the family of God. God had blessed me with many children, Lynette Mulenga's children were three of them.

Pastor Lillian said that we were all going to give God the glory and then sister Melanie was going to pray for every woman individually. That, was another surprise! I hadn't done anything like that before. By now I was trembling and wanted to sit down but Lillian urged me to start speaking in tongues. I had received this wonderful experience five years ago when my Pastor, Dick Monohotoe laid hands on me and I was filled with the Holy Spirit. I spoke in an unknown language which empowered me so much that I knew it was from God. Now here, enveloped with His presence, my speaking became a crescendo of singing in tongues. I so enjoyed being enveloped in His presence that I wasn't aware of anything around me. Pastor Lillian, who was by my left side, brought the women forward and one by one they stood in front of me.

Bursting forth with fire

By now she was holding my left hand up and she said, "Now sister Melanie prophesy."

Not I, but the Holy Spirit of God prophesied and gave me a word of knowledge for each individual woman. My eyes were closed most of the time, but I opened them intermittently when each woman was in front of me. I would look at her face for a moment before closing my eyes again. Although I was in the presence of God I could hear some of the women weeping and I was aware that some had fallen to the floor, others began to speak in tongues and others started to sing praises to God.

I ministered to the first fourteen women rapidly and took a deep breath and asked the Lord Jesus to help me. As the twenty eighth women had been ministered to, all I could do was weep because the whole thing was so supernatural. The time had passed quickly. When I composed myself and can only say "came down to earth," I felt quite exhausted but extremely happy and full of joy. Pastor Lillian said that it was time for some refreshments of tea, coffee and biscuits. Soon after, the women began to leave one by one but as they did, each one shook my hand and curtsied, as is the way of the Zambian Christian, to show a sign of respect. The amazing thing was that they told me that only God knew their situation and words of comfort and advice, prophecy, rhema words (words in season) were apt, as only God knew what I said to them was true. It absolutely floored me.

To speak into somebody's life that is of a completely different culture than mine (typically English), would have been a complete impossibility unless it was from a supernatural Holy Spirit power. Here I was, bursting forth with fire of the Holy Spirit. I was in awe and overwhelmed at being used by God to minister to His children in Kitwe, Zambia. When everyone was leaving, I presented each lady with a silk scarf, twenty-eight in all, the exact number I had brought. When they had gone Pastor

Lillian hugged me and kissed me. She congratulated me on 'bursting forth with fire' and bringing words from God.

I was given the names, addresses and telephone numbers of all the women so that I would remember to pray for them on our return to the U.K. Our church had raised up and supported these two doctors who had given up their good careers so that they could serve the Lord back home in Zambia.

Saturday

After the ladies meeting we returned to Lillian and Joseph's home for a meal and well-deserved good night's sleep. We were exhausted. Next morning we were up early to enjoy the cooler air. We sat chatting around the breakfast table.

"I hear you ladies had a good time last night at the women's meeting, so I am inviting you and Freda to come and speak in the church on Sunday." Joseph waited for our response. Both Freda and I were again taken aback because we hadn't much experience of addressing a congregation or even doing a 'preach' from the bible. I immediately replied,

"Yes, thank you so much," as Freda nudged me sharply in the ribs saying,

"We shall pray about it."

Pray we did because Freda said she could not do it and I had said yes but really I couldn't do it nor did I want to. I think sometimes there is such pride in me, I didn't want to fail or let myself or others down. My stomach was churning just at the thought of it. I was beginning to regret agreeing. Why couldn't I just be truthful and say no? Because Lillian had said God had sent us with a word, I had believed her, and that not to worry because the Holy Spirit would fill our mouths with the right words. Hadn't He already done so, albeit to my surprise.

Pastor Joseph and Lillian had suggested that they would take us to look around Kitwe town. We were excited as we climbed into the car. It was quite a bustling market town and I was pleased because local produce markets always interest me.

The variety of fruits and vegetables was a kaleidoscope of colour and an explosion of smells that delighted the senses. Then came the aromatic smells of the different coloured spices, all piled up on little pieces of cloth. Another table boasted freshwater fish of all descriptions and types that I had never seen before, of course we were a long way from the sea. Then I gazed all around at the ramshackle buildings making up the town. They seemed dark in comparison to the riot of colour in the market place. The shops were so designed to be in the shade to keep them cool. Everywhere was dusty.

Women were selling a beautiful array of materials and you could get measured up for an outfit and it would be ready the next day. I enquired about the cost and was shocked to learn that it would be the equivalent of a few English pounds. I couldn't resist and had my measurements taken. I perused the fabrics and after a while I chose a blue, green and yellow leaf pattern, a traditional African design. The outfit was to be a long skirt with a cap-sleeved top. They gave me some extra fabric to make a scarf headpiece but I didn't wear it as I thought that it would be more appropriate to wear on the Sunday for church and for when I got home. However, the outfit wasn't to be completed until the Monday as they didn't work on Sundays.

After our visit to the market we were taken to the Dayspring Children's Centre which had been set up by John and Michelle Seddon from Kings church in Little Lever, Bolton. They were in partnership in supporting Dr. Joseph and Lillian Mwila. The vision was to help the homeless street children of Kitwe. I had seen a few of them around the market area that morning, begging for money. Some were sat in the rubble of the derelict parts of the town, some looked rebellious and wild, others looked downcast and depressed but in both scenarios you could sense a spirit of hopelessness.

The Dayspring Centre didn't have beds to accommodate the children in the beginning, but they could come for a meal once a day. I watched on as they hurriedly devoured the bowls of food put before them. Some had very swollen bellies, others had their ribs sticking out. Goodness knows what some of the little girls had suffered. We knew that some of the boys were thieves but only God knows what they had seen or experienced in their young lives.

Then for an hour they could receive a bit of education in the Centre. It was on that guise that I was invited to teach them about Jesus. I really enjoyed that because the wild, little boys sat down to listen and the abandoned, abused little girls listened as I told them about the love of God and that Jesus said,

"Suffer the little children to come unto me." (Math.19 v.14) That means let the little children come to me and don't stop them for the kingdom of heaven belongs to such as these. Two boys and a girl responded after being asked if they wanted to give their hearts to Jesus. I was ecstatically happy because here, for me, were the first fruits of Zambia who I had led to the Lord. Soon we had to leave the Dayspring Centre to the mamas who cared for them and returned to the Mwila's for our evening meal and a time of fellowship.

Back to reality and a plate of chips!

We were all up bright and early, washed, dressed and sat down to a delicious breakfast of bananas, pineapple and shema (a porridge-like texture made from maize meal). Freda and I were ushered into a four by four vehicle along with Joseph and Lillian. They took us to a government style building which was set in a big compound. It wasn't until I saw the big placard that I realized that this was a big church and this was where I was going to "preach." Now I started to get really anxious!

We entered this building, which was like an enormous theatre. When I saw how big it was and how high the platform was, I froze to the spot. The auditorium was huge, with about five hundred seats arranged in a semi-circle facing the stage. Row by row the people were flooding in. We were escorted down to the very front row to sit next to the Mwila pastors and several other visiting pastors and their wives. Pastor Joseph got up to pray the opening prayer and named every visitor, giving us an honouring welcome. We sang a couple of songs which seemed to go on forever, along with their shuffling dance in the pews and then Freda and I were invited up on the stage, given a microphone and invited to introduce ourselves. Freda was first. She spoke beautifully then quickly left the stage and sat down back on the front row looking up at me.

By this time, I was shaking at the knees and even thought I would hyperventilate especially when Pastor Joseph said I had a word from God. I felt like a fraud because I had no word from God. Yes, I could quote bible scripture and give my testimony but I really didn't have a direct word from God. I just stood there, quite stunned and then I lifted my eyelids, looked at the multitude of people and scanned the panoramic view of a sea of black faces, with all eyes looking back at me. It was very, very scary. Once I saw their faces I felt a rush of boldness come over me and I could feel the Holy Spirit moving inside my body until a gush of words came forth out of my mouth telling them in a very loud voice,

"God is our Father and He is holy and we are called to be holy. That means to be clean in our thoughts, actions, attitudes and in our behaviour. We who are followers of Jesus Christ who made it possible, by His death and resurrection, for us to have a Father and one that loves us His children, then we should in turn be good fathers and mothers to our children and teach them the ways of our Father God in Heaven."

All was going well until the big crux line came out of my mouth, "To you men of Zambia, why are you creating orphans? We have come all the way from England to feed your orphans. You are an adulterous people who are impregnating lots of women, who are not your wives. Are you drinking, are you smoking? Only the Lord knows if you are. You come to church with all these problems, but you are not to stay the same. If you are truly born again then you can no longer live the secular life of the world.

You have been bought with a high price and that is with the blood of your Saviour who says,

'Without holiness, no-one will see God.' (Heb.12 v 14)

This word from the Lord is to clean up your lives, get down on your knees, ask for forgiveness and start living your lives holy unto the Lord because your Father in heaven knows what goes on in the king's bedchamber".

This is from the bible about Elisha the prophet speaking about the things done and said in secret in the Syrian King's chambers or bedroom, (2 Kings 6 v 8-12).

Well, you could hear a pin drop! Enough had been said and it was time for me to pray over the people, so I closed my eyes and raised my two arms in the air and called upon God to heal His people in Zambia, of this erroneous spirit of sexual immorality within the church and that Father God would be

"A Father to the fatherless." (Ps.68 v 35).

True fathers would take one wife, look after her and they would raise their children together.

At that, I quickly left the stage and sat down next to Freda who was sitting with her mouth open in disbelief. The people's reaction surprised me because now the ladies were standing up and cheering. The men also stood up in agreement uttering a big amen. It was unbelievable. I wasn't the main speaker and thank God that Pastor Joseph had invited another man who went on to preach a very long sermon. Afterwards there was lots of prayer, repenting, weeping and wailing. This was followed by some lovely African worship and then the service was over. Africans tend not to put a time limit on their meetings so by now we realized that it was late afternoon as we were leaving. Joseph and Lillian took us to a fast-food restaurant for a meal. It seemed a bit of an anti-climax compared to what we had just experienced, but now we were 'back to reality and a plate of chips!!' The two pastors were very happy with the day and the way the service had gone. I couldn't believe I had only been there for three days and ministered three times.

Chapter 16

We couldn't afford any of it!

The next day Freda and I left Kitwe and travelled by coach to Lusaka to visit Mutale, Jessie and their children. Mutale was the brother of Lynette Mulenga. We stayed in a nearby lodge and Jessie came to visit us there. She said she would like to take us to the town of Livingstone which is on the Zimbabwe border and where the famous Victoria Falls are. The last time I was in Zambia was with Lynette and she had promised to take me to visit the Falls and to see the ever-present rainbow. Unfortunately, it didn't happen because she passed away in 2000 and it was now 2003.

The next morning came and I felt prompted in my spirit not to wait for Jessie but to quickly go to the coach station and book coach seats to Livingstone for Freda and I. Time in Zambia was running out. I am so glad when the spirit prompts me as it is always the right thing to do. One may say I take risks, big chances or opportunities but I call them divine promptings.

I looked out of the coach window that was to take us to Livingstone, to see Jessie's face looking up at me. Her two children stood either side of her and a family friend called Tom stood behind. I had to go and explain.

"Sorry Jessie, but Freda and I cannot wait one more day to go to Livingstone. If we don't go now it won't be possible to go at all. You promised to take us but we did not hear from you. Maybe we will see you there. Goodbye and God bless."

It took six hours to get to Livingstone, the road was straight, with the bush on each side. Now and then there was a little transit town where the coach would stop for loo's and drinks.

Charles Zulu and Jane (friends of Dr.J.Mwila) were going to be there to meet us. While we were on the coach Charles rang to confirm we were on the way. God's timing is perfect, I had lost Charles's number!! Charles was the manager of Plafours Tours in Livingstone. He had arranged for us to stay at the Rite Inn. Freda and I were delighted because it had a small pool and a swim was just what we needed after that long journey, as we were very tired. They said goodnight and told us that they would return the next morning to work out an agenda for the tour for the Falls and a safari. Then we had to work out how many kwatcha's we had. Aghhh, we couldn't afford any of it! Freda and I went for a late-night swim under the stars, to ease the disappointment

It just happened that it was the night of an eclipse of the moon. We felt excited about being outdoors to witness this spectacular and meaningful event. After the swim and a good night's sleep we would, as they say, "see what the morning brings." Breakfast was at seven thirty and Charles and his colleague Mwansa arrived bright and early. Now how are we to approach the situation I wondered? We had to tell it as it was.

"We don't want to offend you or embarrass ourselves but we are not tourists and we have just come back from being out in the bush etc. Unfortunately, we have little money and cannot afford a tour. We can't even afford a taxi so we are going to catch a bus to the Victoria Falls." There, it was said!

Mwansa listened intently and Charles said nothing. Then they said they would give us a lift to the Falls in their car, it was about ten kilometres out of town and would return to pick us up about twelve noon. We couldn't believe our ears, we were going. After escorting us to the entrance area near the Falls they said goodbye and said that they would collect us later.

Over the rainbow

I could hardly believe it. We're here! It was a dream come true. I was so looking forward to seeing the rainbow over the Victoria Falls, just as much as the cascading water. My first glimpse of the water was through the trees and I could hear the roars of the mighty "Mosi oa Tunya," (the smoke that thunders). I was so excited that I shouted,

"Hallelujah Lord."

Then I heard screams of agony as Freda fell on the first step of the Falls. It was really bad. She'd slipped having not seen the first step as our eyes were fixed expectantly on the water through the trees. Her leg was badly grazed but she was keen to go on. We descended the steps carefully as the mighty waters revealed their full glory to us on our right-hand side. We stopped intermittently at the viewing points to take in this awesome phenomenon of nature. We walked over a narrow bridge which went straight across the waters. I had not seen the rainbow yet.

After continuing around the route, we stopped to eat our picnic and take in the view. We could see the Victoria Falls road bridge that spanned the deep gorge and were over-awed by the enormity of it all, when suddenly someone jumped off the bridge and dangled at the bottom of the gorge on a rope. It was a bungee jumper. We were enthralled watching as one after another leapt into the air, hands out-stretched as if to fly. We later walked over that bridge that led to the Zimbabwe border. We paused to watch a seventy year old woman take her false teeth out and jump! I could hardly believe my eyes. I was frightened just to look over the bridge and down into the raging river. Retracing our steps back through the Falls park I felt a bit disappointed that I hadn't seen the beautiful rainbow that the Falls created as the burning African sun shines on the waters. I had no sooner expressed my disappointment to Freda when a shout of glee came from Freda's lips,

"Look Melanie, look there's the rainbow."

Over the rainbow

I looked up to where she was pointing and sure enough under the narrow iron bridge were the most vivid rainbows, not just one, but two. 'We were over the rainbow.' By now I was so emotional I cried, my childhood dream had come true. I was now 'somewhere over the rainbow way up high' and where dreams really do come true. We were so high up on the pedestrian bridge that the prisms of the rainbow were below us, bowed and arched like the ceiling of a great cathedral, expressing the majesty and glory of this, God's creation and one of the wonders of the world.

A surprise

True to their word Charles Zulu and Mwansa picked us up from the Falls. They took us not back to the lodge as expected, but on a safari, what a surprise. On the way we learned a little more about these kind people. Charles was a very affable man and very gently spoken. He told us that he was a deacon in the church and a long-time friend of Dr. Mwila. They had been at school together in Kitwe. He said he had been a Christian for many years and knew about the work of the Falconer Children's Home. He wanted to show the appreciation of the Zambian people for sending people to help look after their orphans. He was in awe of the fact that we had visited Kebulamema, even he hadn't been there. He said that he and his wife were looking after three orphans from the area of Livingstone where he lived. Mwansa explained that she was a single parent with two children and she loved working with Charles in the tourist industry.

Within less than an hour we arrived at Mosi-oa-Tunya safari park. We entered by crossing over the Zambesi river and the minute we passed through the gates and over the bridge we were driving on a dirt track which ran parallel to the river.

Suddenly a big bull elephant ascended up the riverbank and stopped on the track right in front of the car. It was scary, oh my goodness, what a moment in time that was! That big daddy elephant looked very angry as he stopped to look at us. Torrents of water poured off his grey, thick skinned and magnificent body, his ears flapped and with his trunk raised up high, trumpeted very loudly. Charles warned us that it was not a good sign. He stopped the car so as not to intimidate the creature. It was amazing. As the elephant, was showing his anger, he curled his trunk around a tree and shook it violently, then realizing that we were not posing a threat, stamped off into the thick bush. Once he had gone Charles sighed with relief, (after all we were in a private car, not a jeep), and he said, "It's okay, let's move on."

The next animal we encountered was a tall male giraffe who was feeding from the tops of the trees to our right. As we passed by we could see a whole family group of giraffes. I noticed that some of the giraffes had lost their markings, Charles said it was due to a lack of a certain foliage in the bush. Then we came upon a vast open plain where, quite a way in the distance, we could see a herd of buffalo. Charles said that we would drive closer to them to get a better view and some pictures. I didn't think it was such a good idea really as there were a lot of them. Coming off the track and onto the plain the car stalled and stopped dead. Yes, of course the buffalo looked up and then, oh my days, they began to stampede, in our direction! We had to get out and push the car, all the time looking to the left at the oncoming herd. What a relief when the car started up. We could hear the buffalo snorting and smell the sweat from their backs in the air. My heart was pounding. Charles managed to turn the car around and drove onto the embankment. Freda meanwhile had covered her eyes and was praying hard, very hard. We laughed about it afterwards as we drove along the riverbank, but then we cut into the bush again.

We came across a white rhinoceros. Charles informed me that he was very rare and protected. Would you believe that poachers came in helicopters to steal the rhinoceros? They would shoot them with a stun gun then tie them and airlift them off the reserve. We were looking at this one remaining rhino who they called Gumboot (I have no idea why). He looked so docile that I felt I could have got out and touched him. However, I was advised not to as rhinos can be very aggressive. He was a grey-white colour and just stood grazing on a straw-like plant. He was a sight for sore eyes.

Gumboot the Rhino

As we drove around we encountered zebra, impala, wild boar, and a variety of birds including some very big buzzard like birds, maybe vultures. I remember that they looked very scraggy and as though they were waiting for death and a final feeding frenzy. I certainly didn't want it to be me!

After all that exhilarating fear and excitement Charles and Mwansa told us that this was still not the end of our tour. Freda and I were booked on The African Queen steam boat and that we would eat tea on it as we cruised down the Zambesi river. I was absolutely thrilled having only heard about this trip. As we boarded Charles told us that this was a replica boat, the old one had gone into dry dock and would probably go to a museum. The famous African Queen steam river boat was built in 1912, in the UK for the British East Africa Railway. It was originally named "Livingstone" after the renowned missionary and pioneer David Livingstone. She was used to transport hunters, mercenaries and cargo along the Ruki river for fifty years. (Wikipedia)

The boat set off at a slow leisurely pace. As we cruised down the river what a view we had of ginormous crocodiles partly hidden by the riverbanks, excellent sightings of tall giraffes chomping away at leaves and we saw an astounding variety of large birds which flew over the boat. What I loved best were the small groups of little hippopotamuses basking on the sandbanks in the idyllic afternoon sunshine. Every now and then they would yawn and expose their huge teeth. The boat got so close to them it was surreal. It wasn't a long trip, maybe an hour or so each way but it was fascinating. What a wonderful way to say thank you to us. Freda and I felt honoured. We didn't need appreciation as we were already in great admiration of Mama Lilias Falconer's work which had been the reason for our whole visit.

After one more night in the lodge we took the coach back to Lusaka and then the flight home. What a trip that was and because of it all, my friend Lynette Mulenga's dream to take me to see the Victoria Falls and the rainbow came true.

The Rev. Carol Burstow visiting the leper colony at Tirupati. The pastor who is sitting down has no fingers, toes or nose.

Chapter 17

Opportunity and adventure

The doors were opening fast and furious. The Lord had sent many people onto my pathway to teach me more about ministry and all the time I was learning to trust in the Lord more and more, and to rely on the Holy Spirit of Jesus Christ to fill my mouth with His words. I never really know where the Lord is going to send me next but when the doors of opportunity open He will show me the right one to walk through.

When this next door of opportunity opened for me to be part of a team going to India, I walked through it with confidence. The team was led by the Rev. Carol Burstow from North Wales and she had been going to Andhra Pradesh and Tamil Nadu to work with a Christian group in a leper colony. Rev. Carol is a teacher of the bible and a preacher. She is well-known in many countries for her teaching abilities because most of her life she has been a headmistress in a private school in London. She had reached her seventieth birthday at the time of going out on this next trip.

She invited me along to be a part of her team who would be addressing a women's conference, presenting sketches and ministering to the people in prayer and healing. Rev. Carol always did an altar call which means that she asked if there was anyone who would like Jesus to forgive them their sins and invite Him into their heart and commit their lives to Him. In the many, many meetings thousands of people responded. Rev. Carol worked alongside the local pastors and bishops of different denominations. I have witnessed the amazing responses of people who have surrendered their life to Christ and have been filled with the Holy Spirit and also had the privilege of moving into the throngs to pray for their afflictions. A lot of women who worked in the rice paddy fields had terrible distortions of their spines, hips, knees and feet because they worked in the water-logged paddy fields all day long. It really was quite horrendous that these young women had to suffer so much pain from this tiresome work and many of them had to carry their babies along with them. After the initial shock of so many people coming forward for prayer, we called upon the Holy Spirit and spoke in a heavenly language until many of them got healed. Some of them cried and shouted out with glee as the pain left their bodies. This was an occurrence we found everywhere we went and on every trip.

The team comprised of, Rev. Carol, Sue Dray, Thelma Lynch (a good friend), Rachel, Kelly, Warren and I. One of the team, a lady, Sue Dray, from Oldham spoke on Pro-Life and how God hates abortion. She would speak very graphically about the procedure of aborting a baby and the devastating effects on both the baby and the mother. In India they prefer boys and still abort girls. Within the casting system girls can have a tough life and women in any position are looked down upon.

Rev. Carol comes from an Anglican background. She stands six feet tall, is very matriarchal, speaks the Queen's English with authority as a head teacher and a Minister of the Church. I felt very comfortable going with Rev. Carol and very privileged to be invited. As I walk by faith and not by sight I didn't need to know a lot about where I was going to sleep or eat, or about the towns and cities we were going to visit, or about the people we would meet. Rev. Carol had been there many times and I felt very safe. I wanted to serve God by serving her and help her in any way I could. After the flight I knew that we had to take a long train journey across India and that for me, it was going to be an exciting adventure.

We arrived at Chennai airport after a nine hour flight to be met, with a very warm welcome, by Pastor Gali, who guided us to the train station where we caught the early morning train to Tirupati, which is a city in the Indian State of Andhra Pradesh. Just being at the station was an experience, it was heaving with people. Some had put down mats and were fast asleep as they waited for their trains. I marvelled at how they managed to sleep amid the noise and multitudes of feet almost trampling them. We waited patiently for our train to arrive. It was heralded by a whistle as it approached. Our train, one of those magnificent, British built steam trains, slowly pulled into the platform along with an overwhelming aroma of excrement, for the train toilets were a hole in the floor and the excrement just fell in between the lines. People were hanging onto the doors and descended in a wild stampede before the train rumbled to a stop. At Tirupati we were met by Pastor Sam from Madurai who accompanied us for the next two days. Pastor Gali took us to his house where we met his lovely wife and family and the orphans he cares for. Then we went on to our humble hotel where we rested after our long journey.

Visits

That evening we drove to a nearby village where we preached to the people, many of whom received the gospel eagerly. The following day we went to Pastor Gali's house again where we met a mighty man of God, the Rev. Meyers, who had been instrumental in establishing a leper colony, ministering to the needs of many lepers and stamping out leprosy there. We had a wonderful conversation with this servant of the Lord, who, well into his eighties and had spent his life working with the underprivileged in India. Only a few hours later we heard that Rev. Meyers had died – his last word being "Jesus." That evening we returned to the leper colony to have a service and to comfort the people who had lost someone very close to their hearts. Strangely Rev. Carol looked like his wife who had died two years earlier and this seemed to help the sorrow of the people.

The next day we visited a school and shared bible stories and drama with the children. Then we visited a children's prison where there were boys from seven to seventeen. They were kept in very stark conditions but were delighted when, after the ministry, we presented them with yo-yo's, cars and balloons. Hopefully our visit did something to alleviate the pitiful conditions in which the boys found themselves.

The following day we visited a women's prison where we spoke with five prisoners about the love of Jesus, then it was on to a secondary school which was run by a Christian headmaster and Christian staff. We took an assembly for about three hundred girls and we were able to do little sketches about The Good Samaritan (Luke 10 v.25-37) which were well received. Then we spoke about how we should love the unlovable, help each other and prefer others needs first.

The next morning was the start of the two day women's conference. As we entered the room over two hundred women were sitting cross-legged on the ground waiting for us. So many ladies had turned up to hear the Good News of the gospel that Pastor Gali had to take off the door so that the people, including some men who were outside, could listen and catch some of the messages that Rev. Carol and the team were preaching. Many people received the Holy Spirit during that conference. There is a hunger for the things of God in India and many Hindus are coming to the Lord as the Holy Spirit moves over Asia.

The day after we ministered to about a hundred pastors at the pastor's conference where they were eager for all of God that we could share.

One evening we paid a visit to the Fox people (they eat foxes!). It turned out to be quite a wild time. They lived in igloo-shaped tents at the side of the road. There were a lot of toddlers and children amongst them. The grown-ups were screaming, fighting and shouting at each other. It was quite harrowing as we were told that the young men carried knives and there was a tribal war going on. It was very difficult to gain their attention, so we sung some Christian songs and did a sketch about Jesus healing the demonic man and how the demons went into the pigs (Mark 5 v 1-13). That caught their attention and was relevant to them as there were a lot of piglets running around.

Roaming freely were large cows with big horns, which are considered to be holy by the Hindus. You could not touch them because the Hindu's believed that they are sacred. You could be arrested or stoned. It was very dark and another fight broke out between some of the teenagers who had knives. It became quite violent as they were shouting and jeering at another group of boys. At that point we left, in a hurry!

We also had an opportunity to go to talk and pray with the people who were sleeping on the streets in Tirupati. They are considered to be homeless people but they like to be where the night action is, that action being drug dealing and prostitution.

Train journeys

It was time to leave Tirupati, a town known in India as a place of pilgrimage to the god Vishnu, but we believe that our God Jehovah is making an impact there. We travelled overnight by train, a fourteen hour journey, to Kottayam in Kerala where a lady called Celine had arranged another women's conference for the team to conduct. Celine had cut down many trees at the back of her house to create a covered area for the conference. Celine had several orphans living at her house and provided food, clothing and education for them.

The ladies and some pastors came to the conference and God moved powerfully through the preaching and teaching. Warren, Kelly, Sue and Rachel ministered to about a hundred children, no easy matter in the hot temperatures.

With the conference over it was time to return to Chennai, involving another long train journey. Most Indians travel by train as the network, built by the British, is extremely reliable and convenient. We took the opportunity to rest and slept very well. In Chennai we had a meeting with Pastor Eva's daughters who minister to the prostitutes and sex workers, some of whom have been Hindu temple prostitutes. The ladies received the messages we brought to them gladly and there was a lot of love in the service.

Rev. Carol treated the whole team to a beautiful buffet at the Meridian hotel as a thank you before they left. It was extremely welcome after the pollution we had seen and the curries of the previous days!! The salubrious surroundings showed us how rich India could live, in stark contrast to the poverty we had seen every day.

Sadly it was now the hour for Thelma and I to leave them and travel to Gunter District in Andhra Pradesh to view the orphanage built and supported by The Sunflower Trust.

Thelma and I visiting the orphanage.

We had another six hour train journey through the night and we arrived in Tenali to be met by Pastor Gyri who runs the orphanage with his wife Jerusha. What a rural place this was, with oxen, water buffalo, wart hogs, and other wildlife abounding in the streets. In this area many people had never seen a white person, so we were an immediate attraction wherever we went. A network of about ten pastors worked in unity in all the villages covering the vast area in Gunter district. Every day we travelled many miles on remote roads and muddy tracks to minister in different churches. The people were delighted to receive us, the first foreigners to ever go to some of these places. We sung, preached, performed drama, gave testimonies and shared God's love with the people. As there were only the two of us, we had to depend on God to fill our mouths with living words for the people who were hungry for the teaching. Every day God sent a shower of rain before we arrived and at a time of year which normally has no rain, this was looked on as a blessing because we had come.

One evening we were so tired that they sent us to a believer's house where they brought beds out into the garden for us to sleep a while under the stars. We thanked the Lord for a light blanket so that the mosquitos could not get too much supper!!

On the final day of our trip Pastors Gyri and Paul took us to the village of Bhattiprolu where thirty orphans were waiting to greet us with flowers and singing. What a beautiful bunch of children, all being educated by Pastor Gyri. He is such a man of vision and has started building a new place for the orphanage and the church. He is believing for ten to twenty water buffalo (each costing £200-£250), so that he can sell the milk and make the orphanage self-sufficient. Then we were taken on a trip down the Krishna river in a large wooden boat. It was like paradise and we saw fish jumping out of the water and all kinds of wildlife.

At the beginning of the trip Thelma had given out a prophetic word about the river, flowing in India for God's Indian Bride and that the people should jump into the river to swim with the Spirit of God. It was amazing to end up on the last day cruising down the river to the Bay of Bengal. On the way back we sang praises with the pastors in the boat and the captain asked us to pray for him.

Well, the final day arrived and we sadly left India for the trip back to Heathrow, part of our hearts have been left with the beautiful Indian people.

Melanie and the water buffalo

As I write I am pleased to say that we raised the money for several water buffalos which went on to provide the orphanage with an abundance of milk as water buffalo can be milked three times a day. There was plenty of milk left over to sell and use to support the orphanage.

Chapter 18

Looking back

There can be no summing up in this book. As the time goes on and on, so does the work. Recently I have been looking at my endless files, for every trip has been recorded in one way or another. My tally is of visits to at least fifty countries, some more than once and some multiple times.

"For you created my inmost being, you knit me together in my mother's womb (Psalm 139 v.13)

"all the days ordained for me were written in your book before one of them came to be" (Psalm 139 v.16)

God knew that I would always want to travel. He placed me in a foster home where Doris, the foster mother's daughter had married Eric, a sergeant in the army. They travelled to Cyprus, Singapore, Germany and India and Doris would always send me letters or photographs about the country she was in. My sister Rose and I made a wonderful stamp collection. The stamps and pictures stirred my imagination and I dreamed that one day I would go to these exotic places. At school I excelled in geography, writing essays about the countries Doris had visited. I remember my best essay was about tea that was grown in India. Doris had sent me a tea leaf along with pictures of the women in the fields picking the tea leaves. Another was an essay about olives and olive oil that she observed being processed in Cyprus. Doris had been a librarian and she helped with my education more than she will ever know.

Only God Himself sent me to the countries I visited. Before I became a Christian and when I was younger, I had been taken by train to Spain. Travelling through France was wonderful, the diversity of the scenery was stunningly different. Torremolinos in Spain was our destination. It was still a fishing village in those days, there were no sky-scraping hotels, bars, or restaurants invading the beach area. We stayed in a small lodge. It was like heaven on earth, I delighted in the scenery around me. I didn't go abroad for many years after that because I entered the School of Life. I married into a Travelling community at the age of fourteen and was soon raising a family.

With hindsight I can see how Father God was training me for what lay ahead. When my children had grown up, I had holidays in Yugoslavia and Spain with my husband. It was not always a pleasant experience as he just liked to drink himself into a stupor along with our travelling companions. It was on holidays to Malta and Cyprus where I went sight-seeing, that I found locations and archaeological sites that were mentioned in the Bible about the Apostle Paul's missionary journeys. He had visited both countries, been shipwrecked in Malta in St. Paul's Bay and sailed with Barnabas from Antioch (Turkey) to Salamis in North Cyprus, where they taught in the synagogues about Christ's salvation. I wasn't a believer at that point, but I have always been interested in history, architecture, art and music. All these things left a lasting impression on my mind, but I wondered if they were true as I looked at them through the eyes of a tourist. I did not realize how meaningful and enlightening they would be to me further down the line of my life.

God Himself was educating me and gently introducing me to His Son Jesus. What a wonderful journey it has been too. Like Paul, I have been shipwrecked and in many a tempest but looking back, I can see that my Saviour God saved me, delivered me and directed me. His Spirit was working on my lively mind and later His words dropped into my heart and finally into my spirit. Once my spirit was awakened to The Truth and I surrendered my life, then I was able, by His goodness and grace to embark on my incredible journeys or as I call them, "Mission Trips." I was and still am, on a mission to speak, to proclaim the Good News about Jesus, God and the Holy Spirit.

In October 1988 I was Born Again, on June 17th 1989 I married my common-law husband John, in Emmanuel Church

Manchester and in September 1989, along with our three children, we were all baptised. The Lord ordained it and I obeyed. Now I was fit for purpose. I didn't know very much, but the Holy Spirit has taught me everything and Jesus has loved me, cared for me and given me authority in His Name, (not my name, for I am nobody). Knowing that the Almighty God was truly my heavenly Father took me to another level and dimension in the Spirit. This led me to prepare for my first mission/aid trip in 1990 to Romania, which I wrote about in the first chapter.

I have never lost my passion for Jesus or for missions. I am spurred on by His Holy Spirit fire within me, like an urgency to spread the gospel, to feed the poor, and help the widows and orphans.

Romania was the first mandate from God, He gave me a choice, either I believed and did it, or I didn't believe and did nothing. Out of a grateful and willing heart I jumped at the opportunity. I didn't know at that time that my choice would be international and generational. My Father God provided everything. Setting up The Sunflower Trust charity was purely to ensure I never went out empty handed, and I NEVER HAVE.

No matter where I am

God gave me Hungary as a second home and He gave me the nation as an inheritance, along with all my Hungarian 'children' and many little girls have been named after me. He gave me Africa as my joyful playground, where worship and praise was an absolute pleasure. India was a feast to my eyes and showed me the reality of idols that people worshipped, big stone images with grotesque forms and wicked man-made gods. China opened my eyes to the wealth of the Asian continent and also to how they worshipped another 'no god'. Buddhism is originally a philosophy and religious teaching. America showed me how people loved Jesus as I travelled across the bible belt many times. My impression was that the churches were either a very upmarket super-church or a very religious one, although

195

there have now sprung up many spirit-filled churches led by wonderful men and women of God. I did love the Afro-American gospel churches, not only because they were happy and joyful, but they were very spiritual, although it could have seemed like, 'let's enjoy the service' addiction. I don't mean to be critical but just to report my feelings, because those who declare Jesus as their Lord and Saviour and love Him are His children. They too are on a journey and Jesus will direct their path, just as He has done for me. I preach Jesus crucified and that He is the Way, the Truth and the Life. No matter where I am, on a street corner, in a queue, a plane, a bus or a train, I can witness. To see people saved is my purpose in life, but I can only point them in the right direction, that is to the cross.

God knows I was never driven by money because I never had any money. I wasn't driven by power or fame because it was too much to live up to. No, I was driven by the Holy Spirit of God. I had very little education, nor do I have any qualifications either academically or theologically. Most churches I have been to found me to be 'over the top" as a passionate and enthusiastic Christian.

I am very loud in worship, prayer, praising and preaching. I can't help it!! God called me to be a loud Shofar (trumpet), a loud call to be heard, a call for repentance, a call to people to wake up to the reality of Father God and to the sacrificial life of Jesus. Father God made me bold, took away my fear and replaced it with faith. The Holy Spirit directed me to every country that I have visited. I have always been received as a missionary, minister, prophetess, teacher, evangelist and in India and Africa an apostle. None of these titles I ever wanted or could live up to. There would be too much expectation to perform or too much overwhelming honour given, BUT God knows that, and He has used me in every situation.

I co-ordinate, arrange and work for the Lord alongside bishops, pastors and international ministries. I have to organize travel, apply for visas, and check all foreign documentation required. I have run an International ministry and charity for thirty years and I have never had to ask or beg for money. Based on a book I read about George Muller's life and his times of God's provision, I asked God if he would do the same for me. I did raise money once by buying some small crocheted black bags and embroidering little sunflowers on them, then selling them at doors or to friends or at meetings where I would be giving a testimony.

I am part of the Women's Aglow ministry but don't attend many meetings as I am one of their speakers. I have never in thirty years been asked for my credentials. God made me an ambassador of Christ and a servant of the Most High God. This is what keeps me motivated and hopefully humble. In all these years God has been my provider, Jehovah Jireh. During my early ministry I still had to go out to work every day to buy food and pay for gas and electricity for my family. God blessed me every day and in every season.

God of possibilities

On one occasion I gave my testimony in my home church in Little Lever, Bolton. A lovely Irish lady had come to visit some friends on that particular day and although we didn't meet, she went back to Belfast and told a friend about me. He was a, teacher in her children's school. She must have expounded my story very well as he asked her to get my phone number. Indeed, he rang me a week or so later. I wasn't too sure what he wanted but soon established that he wasn't a believer. His name was Don McBurney and he was affiliated to UNESCO at that time, through A Ray of Hope which organises international art, music, festivals and competitions promoting the talents of children. He asked me a lot of questions. After he had looked at the Sunflower Trust website, I think he concluded that I was a credible person. In fact he said,
"It's incredible what you are doing as an individual and as a voluntary aid worker, feeding poor children, looking after

orphans in India, Hungary and Romania with no church, charity, ministry or organisation supporting you."
I quoted from Phil.4 v.19
"My God supplies all my needs according to His riches in glory."
At that, he changed the subject!

During a later conversation he asked me where my next destination was. Well, at that time I was planning to go to India again. I was going to take a team of people with me. I explained that some time ago I had been contacted by an Indian pastor asking for some prayer and assistance after the Tsunami that had hit the East coast of India in 2004. It was the first time I had heard the word Tsunami. The media had shown the most catastrophic images of great devastation and death. I can only say that the Spirit of God prompted me to answer the call and act upon it.

Firstly, I was able to send monetary relief via The Sunflower Trust, then I gathered some like-minded people together and started to pray about how to help this pastor of a small village in Andhra Pradesh, India. As we communicated via the internet, I had a clear picture of his vision which was to take on three orphans whose parents had died in the Tsunami. We actually took on thirty-three! Now we wanted to build an orphanage and children's home in Andhra Pradesh. The Lord miraculously provided the money to make the bricks.

I had been asked by a stranger to come to her house and pray for her. She had a very difficult problem and she believed that my prayers for her would be answered and they were. She sent a cheque as a thank you for a thousand pounds and included a note to say that she wouldn't trouble me again. I didn't know if she was a believer and I never saw her again. I sent the money out to the pastor and another miracle happened. The building workers were all free in the month of August and they worked for no pay!

Just to add that the orphanage was completed in 2007, housing Pastor Babu, his wife, three children, two cooks/housekeepers and the orphans. Later the upper floor was made into a church that could hold more than one hundred and fifty people. It is still functional today.

Completely out of the blue Mr. McBurney said he would give me a free ticket!! Well, I was astonished. In previous years, only once before had someone paid for my flight. As I have already said I never take any money out of the Trust, though I could quite justifiably do so. The Trust couldn't afford it, it rarely had more than a couple of hundreds of pounds in it at any one time. The money is for the Lord's work. Even expenses I incur gladly and with a joyful heart. God has always given me exactly what I need. Mr. McBurney told me that every year British Airways donated ten airline tickets to him to give to a worthy charity. For the next five years he gave me one each year. I went to India and Africa twice, and the final one I had a choice of Pakistan or Bangladesh. I chose to go to Bangladesh because I had an ulterior motive.

Sharing the love of Jesus with the street children in Dhaka

Washing the feet of the disciples

Chapter 19

Do it afraid

I had done my homework about Bangladesh and I could see that my father's village was just over the border in India. Oh, how I longed to meet my father's people, my own blood relatives. My father had been dead now for fifty years. I thanked God for this opportunity because I knew I could travel that hundred or so miles across the border. I also knew that my brother had family in Sylhet, east Bangladesh. It was possible, my God is a God of possibilities. I had to go alone as no-one else could afford a ticket of eight hundred pounds.

I was excited and a little afraid but I remembered a Joyce Meyer quote from her book, Do it afraid (1996 Warner Books) 'If you are afraid, DO IT AFRAID anyway.'
Adventure and excitement sums me up really!

I had a lovely contact in Dhaka and was invited to stay at the Baptist Bible Faculty of Dhaka, in the student accommodation. It was holiday time and there were no students in residence. The first week I worked with the pastors who introduced me to a ministry called "The Sacrifice Trust," a wonderful group of young people who sung for the Lord. They were amazing worshipers in a Muslim county. I was surprised at how they were quite free to hold church and evangelise. The leaders were young men and women who loved to perform the ceremony of feet washing. (John 13 v. 3-17). I was invited to the school for the blind, to preach and teach with them and to join the pastors in their ministry to the street kids of which there are thousands. By God's grace I was able to pray over and with young ministers and their children. They brought me food every day but sometimes I was invited to believer's homes for meals.

The big church denominations were present but the Born Again churches were mainly held in people's homes, as in the days of the Apostles. I can't say if people gave their lives to Jesus but I spoke the simple and pure gospel wherever I went.

The second week was about pursing my family heritage. I didn't ever want to die before seeing my father's people. I would know then exactly who I was, who my people are and if the stories that I had heard were correct. Now if it was possible I could go and find the truth. My late father's people would see me and know me, the second daughter of Ataur Rahaman, whose grandfather Lutfa was a high-ranking Imam. My father had a town named after him, Ma-Ataurah and I wanted to go there.

The first part of the week I was to go to visit some of my brother's friends and family in Narsingdi, a city about forty miles east of Dhaka by coach. The coach was crowded with people pushing and shoving to get on. I had my ticket and although my Christian brothers wanted to go with me, I felt it was wiser to go alone as the family were Muslims and it could have been dangerous for the men. After all I was just a woman dressed in my sari with my head covered, and looking very insignificant, so less of a threat. The Christian brothers insisted on calling or texting me every hour or so on my mobile to make sure I was O.K. (Thank God for mobile phones). God was in all this and although it was the most irresponsible decision I had ever made, I knew my Father God, my Jesus and His Holy Spirit would guard, guide and direct me.

The family

Arriving in Narsingdi, Momen and his wife Popy were there at the coach station to greet me. They were relatives of my brother. Momen was so welcoming and he called for two tuk-tuks to take us to their very humble home in the poorest part of the town. I liked it though. It consisted of one main room and a small kitchen type room, although they did the cooking outside. The building was built of breeze blocks and had a corrugated tin roof which was jammed against the dwelling next door. A little booth-sized outbuilding housed the shower and 'hole in the ground' toilet. There was a lovely little garden at the front of the house that brought a bit of beauty to the eyes. The main room had a very big bed in it and a small dressing table which was covered with souvenirs and artifacts.

Momen was going to stay with his sisters, of which he had five but no brothers. His wife Popy was going to sleep in the bed with me. I was quite happy with this arrangement. Whenever I was in their home I had to lie on the bed and Popy's mum would come in sometimes with fruits or food, but mainly rice, and she would feed me with her hands. This was an honoury custom to elders of the community and I was a related to the family. Popy could speak very good English and was a teacher at the government school which was situated in the middle of a forest. She had a daughter, Mahek, who was about three months old at the time. Popy's uncle lived with them but he was staying somewhere else whilst I was there. He could speak a little English, so I was able to communicate, although their comprehension was something else!

They knew all about my sister Rose and I as my brother had always spoken about his mother and sisters, who he didn't remember, but knew they lived in London, England. His relatives in London had tracked my father and mother's lives, but he only heard things second and third hand.

I enjoyed my short stay with them. I was shown love, respect and honoured as an Aunty. Momen, who couldn't speak English would sit on the edge of the bed cross-legged and rub my feet (which I thoroughly enjoyed) all the time saying, "Auntee, Auntee."
He was very happy to have me in their humble home.

Days Out

Momen took me into the forest on his motor bike to show me Popy's school. The headmaster greeted me warmly and asked if I would like to take a few classes in English and talk about life in the UK, giving the children opportunity to ask questions about our culture and economy. Of course, I obliged enthusiastically and was possibly the instigator of many Bengalis coming to London years later. Popy translated for me.

Momen was a fish breeder and wanted me to see his work, so again clinging to his back I had the journey of my life. Once off the main road he sped through the woods into the forest and stopped in a clearing where there were six or eight pools of water. They looked quite stagnant and green with algae. However, the ponds became alive with large fish jumping out of the water to receive the food which he threw in. It was quite a foray.

Then he took me to visit his five sisters who lived in a little wooden shed nearby. None were married and it was Momen's responsibility to feed them as their parents had died. It was poverty at its lowest point. The girls were happy to see an English lady, but they were very shy and remained behind their veils. It was a most memorable time.

On another occasion Momen, Popy and Mahek took me to the town zoo. It was a bit of a shock. There were different species of monkeys in separate cages which were no bigger than the monkeys. They were very cramped and each one looked at me with sad, sombre eyes, pleading to be let out. When I went too close they became aggressive, can you blame them? There was a lovely brown bear who stood about six feet tall. He was tethered to a big piece of iron by a short metal chain in a barred enclosure. At times the keeper made him dance, I had seen this once in Romania. I hated it. How could they use their animals for entertainment? There were beautiful exotic birds of every colour and description who chirped and sung as we passed by.

I forgot to mention that my hosts in Dhaka had also taken me to the zoo, a much pleasanter place situated near the city. I observed some very strange creatures. Here, the highlight was a giant Indian elephant who was giving rides around a dried mud circuit. I couldn't resist having a turn. I climbed a ladder which was fastened to his side to get onto his back and excitedly waited for another ride of my life. The magnificent animal walked sedately and slowly, the opposite end of the spectrum to the motor bike ride through the forest. Up to this point I had had a rather nice time but now it was time to go on another fact-finding adventure into India.

Ride of my life

A very hot journey

Popy's uncle, her mother's brother, was going to escort me . It was his duty as a man and as women could not travel alone, not because of danger, although that is one aspect, but also because in Muslim countries a woman can only travel with a male family relative. So Mostofa became my nephew escort.

We departed Narsingdi early, about six in the morning, as by mid-day it would be very hot. I dressed in a sari and wore my scarf around my head and put my sunglasses on. I was prepared for the journey. Mostofa and I boarded the bus to a neighbouring town and there we were met by Mr. Alusion, our guide, and we were to be accompanied by five other men. Mr. Alusion had a son in the Isle of White and my brother Manicur had trained him as a chef. Manicur had arranged for Mr.Alusion to take me to Sylhet District on the East India border. They had three vehicles, tuk-tuks, which were like motor bikes with a large rear seat. It was a tight fit and I wasn't very comfortable having Mostofa so close to me, but I had to be grateful that these men were doing this for me quite voluntarily. I think I just paid for the fuel. I was excited, joyful and optimistic when we set off, but as we drove on mile after mile, the heat of the day was rising and I was getting a little irritable. Only Mostofa would ask now and then if I was OK.

"Shister, you OK?" he enquired. He couldn't pronounce sister.

"Yes, OK thank you." I replied.

No-one else could speak to me due to the language barrier and we had a lot of miles to go. Now and then, we stopped for a drink of water which I was very grateful for. I had put a bottle of water in my bag before we left.

The scenery changed at every turning point. After leaving Narsingdi things began to look more rural. It was quite nice really as we drove alongside miles and miles of paddy fields. Bare-chested, dark-skinned coolies were wearing huge sunhats so you couldn't see their faces, but they were protected from the burning sun as they planted rice roots from their little boats. Beyond the paddy fields I could see some mountains and the higher peaks were capped with snow. It brought back a memory of what my mother had told me about my father's people who lived in a beautiful area, in the east of India.

Father had told her that you could see the snow-capped Himalayan mountains in the distance where streams and rivers meandered down its slopes to the valleys below. In the valley were vast expanses of grasses, fruit trees and there were rice fields on the mountain slopes.

She told me that my father and grandfather had worked for the East India Tea company. Grandfather Lutfa was of The

Royal House of India and he was friends with The Viceroy of India, Lord Louis Mountbatten, the Queen's cousin. The British were still in control in my grandfather's day but both he and my father experienced the bloody war as the British Empire exited the country.

My Father's grave site

Chapter 20

Remorse

I was jolted back to reality and realised that I was still cramped in the tuk-tuk and had become both hot and sweaty. Now we were about to ford a river.

The Ferry

We all got out of the tuk-tuks, a great relief and a moment to stretch our legs. The vehicles were driven onto what looked like a large wooden floating platform which had to be pulled manually by ropes to cross to the other side. Looking down the river I could see the old vessel had broken and partly sunk. The river was greenish and murky and certainly didn't entice me to have a swim much as I love swimming. We were transported across and then climbed up to the top of the mud embankment which had been hardened into clay by the fierce, burning sun. There would have been too much weight in the tuk-tuk to have been driven up. The view as I looked back was lovely, but by now I wanted to go home (wherever that was!).

My prayers of thanks for giving me this wonderful opportunity had now turned into prayers of remorse. I began telling God that I was sorry for my selfishness in wanting to meet my father's family and know the truth of what really happened to him. Inside I was wretching and crying as we covered mile after mile of road which had now become bumpy, dirt track paths. After an hour or so we arrived at a small town called Charkari. As we drove through the main thoroughfare with its busy little wooden booths and hut shops, I was amazed to see very westernized clothes for sale like Tee shirts with English logos and sports logos on them. Strange because all the women wore saris and the men wore cotton pyjama-like trousers and tunics as is typical attire in these Muslim countries. Men didn't wear anything colourful. This little town seemed drab and poor to me. The women were small and thin. Their saris were made of a dull coloured cotton so different to those I had seen in Dhaka.

The entourage of tuk-tuks stopped for a while and the men went to buy something from the little shop. Mostofa asked again if I was alright, but other than that no-one else spoke to me. Soon back on the road again, I noticed it was late afternoon and my thoughts turned to where I was going to sleep. Maybe it would be in my father's villa. We travelled on through village after village. In one, I noticed an unusual sight of men playing football. They wore colourful football strips and it was a very pleasant sight, something more normal, as I saw a more relaxed side to these eastern people.

We drew into a little village and stopped outside a small mosque. To my surprise there was a gathering of men waiting for us. One man had a white turban on his head and was dressed in a black tunic, typical of an Imam. They gestured for me to sit down on a chair behind a desk which was situated in front of the door to the mosque. I had expected that at some point people or the authorities would want to know who I was and what I was doing in these far way parts. I didn't expect what happened next.

What have I said, or done?

Mostofa translated for me. They asked me my name and the names of my father and grandfather and mother. I was able to answer confidently. When I had told them they all just stared at me in disbelief. I felt very uncomfortable and afraid but kept my poise and remembered what I was here for. I lowered my eyes as they were all staring and by now some other men had joined them. I was feeling very intimidated but was praying all the time in my head. Suddenly all the men started talking to each other their voices getting louder and louder resulting in complete chaos. They seemed to be arguing and in a bit of a frenzy. Oh my goodness I thought, what have I said or done?

When they had calmed down, they went into the mosque leaving me outside with a few of the men in attendance. After a little while Mostofa came out with one of the men and said,

"No, they don't know anyone by those names and we should return to Narsingdi."

So that, was that. I had come to a dead end but at least I had tried. By now I was tired and hungry. These men hadn't offered me anything to eat or drink. It was early in the evening when we climbed back into the tuk-tuks to begin our journey back. Oh my goodness, the thought of that long, dusty road was not appealing. We set off and after a few miles I noticed it was turning dusk and my thoughts again focussed on where I was going to sleep. We were near Assam on the Indian border so surely we would stop at a lodge to spend the night, or would I be spending the night in my father's eleven bedroomed villa that my mother had told me about? Checking on the villa was his reason for going back twice a year. (At that time my father lived in London with my mother and elder sister). Because I was English, I even wondered if might be given a room at the Maharajah's hotel….my vain imaginations were running wild again! I was completely exhausted.

We travelled a few more miles, dusk had now fallen, the scenery changed into a hazy blur and the dust from the front tuk-

tuk threw up a continuous dust cloud that burned my eyes, my throat and got up my nose. I had had enough. I was just about to insist that they took me back to Narsingdi when the leader turned off the main track onto a tree lined road and into a farmyard.

I couldn't quite make out the structure of the house, but I could see an emaciated cow and a few little goats in front of it and to the left, a figure of a small woman who was sweeping up with a broom made of twigs. All the men got off the tuk-tuks and started speaking in their own language. They seemed happy to be home. Mr. Alusion pulled a large set of keys out of his bag, the sort a prison officer might have. He opened the door and beckoned everyone in. Now I felt very uneasy, this house had obviously been locked up whilst Mr. Alusion had been away. To my horror I realised that the main door was made of thick, heavy metal, like a prison door. Now I was really concerned and a little afraid. All the time I was talking to God in my mind and trying to reassure myself. All I really wanted to do was lie down and go to sleep. I had no choice but to follow on into the building, like a lamb to the slaughter, because there was nowhere else to go.

My stomach was churning

A man gestured for me to walk along the long corridor to a room at the far end. By now it was dark outside and very gloomy inside, another man lit an oil lamp. It was made of clay and shaped just like the ones I had seen in bible pictures. As it lit the room up, I could see that there was a large bed and two chairs. From a gesture and the tone of the man's voice, I was ordered to sit down.

The men were relaxed and laughed together as they talked, whereas I was becoming a nervous wreck. Of course I tried to keep my poise and sat there in silence, trying not to show my fear. I wanted them to go away and leave me alone while I slept on that bed. Yet another man came in with some chai and some exotic fruits. Slowly and with dignity, I ate them. Sooner or later the men would go to sleep as it had been a long day. Mr. Alusion sat on the chair opposite me near the open bedroom door, Mostofa and the other men hovered at the door and in the corridor. There was a different tone in their voices and now Mostofa was nowhere to be seen, so I wasn't able to find out what was happening.

I sat for a moment, then just as I was about to speak, I saw a creature's shadow high up on the wall and right above the bedstead. My face, in the flickering lamp-light, must have said it all, as all the men's eyes were looking at me, then following my stare, to see a floppy rag-like spider, as big as a dinner plate, crawling up the wall. Mr. Alusion gave a shout and a man came with a long duster and swiped it off the wall. The creature fell, either behind or onto the bed. Sweat dropped from my brow and into my eyes which were closing in tiredness. I wanted to sleep, my stomach was churning and now, not knowing the whereabouts of that spider, I knew that in no way could I sleep in that room.

By now I was beside myself and made a gesture with my hands that I needed to sleep. Thankfully Mr. Alusion understood. He shouted and a scarf-covered woman appeared beckoning me to follow her to another room. It was made of stone and concrete and looked very much like a jail. It was lit by an oil lamp and on entering, and with great relief I saw a small bed with a big mosquito net hanging over it from the ceiling. She pointed to the toilet at the rear of the room which was simply a hole in the ground. Well I definitely needed that now! With her hands put together in a prayer-like pose, she bowed very low and left me.

It must have been around ten o'clock and I was thoroughly exhausted, probably mental fatigue contributed to that as well as that tedious journey. The Christian brothers from Dhaka texted me to ask if I was OK. To which I replied, "yes, but please pray for me as I have no idea where I am."

I knew that Mostofa would be in touch with his sister back in Narsingdi and would tell her where we were and what was happening. Their only concern seemed to be if I was eating well and being treated like the Begum Saab (a royal title meaning princess) that I was.

Popy rang me up and asked me how I was. I couldn't speak for long as my phone battery was getting low. I said, "I want to come back to Narsingdi, I don't want to continue. The journey is too much and the terrain is not agreeable to this English lady who usually travels by plane, train, car or ship."
I didn't care anymore about finding my father's estate or my relatives, which I had spent a lifetime dreaming about. Popy replied,
"Please Aunty, don't give up now you are nearly there, just rest and sleep. Within two hours tomorrow you will be there at, Shaistaganj which is in Assam on the Indian border. I really had no idea where I was, it was only after my return home that I could do some research.

I was ready to lie down and stretch out on the bed, but first I had to experience the loo! So, closing my eyes and crouching down I relieved myself. No creatures came scurrying out of the hole, phew! I'd experienced this archaic type of toilet before in Africa, France and Eastern Europe. They always harboured rats and creepie crawlies. Bedtime at last, I used my bag as a pillow and covered my head with a scarf. The mattress was made of pressed straw and there was an aroma of animal permeating through it. I tried to sleep, but I was overtired and my mind was still running riot. Once again I prayed to my Father God and asked him to protect me and help me get through the night. I thanked Jesus for the day and slowly drifted off to sleep. It wasn't a deep sleep because after what seemed a short time I heard the sound of feet coming down the corridor.

And that's where it seemed I was.

There were many feet coming down the stone corridor and immediately a great fear came over me. I thought the worst, they've come to kill me, or even worse molest me or hold me for ransom. I'm dead!! It's my own fault Lord I should never have come. All these thoughts swirled round my head. Dear Jesus, let it be quick, please don't let them touch me, or torture me.

By the time the men arrived at the door of my room I felt like I was hyperventilating.......They entered the room from the right and one man shouted,

"Butt, butt madame, butt."

I didn't know what it meant and by now I didn't care, all I knew was that I was one Christian woman in a locked building with these Muslim men and they had all come into my room. I shouted to them to get out but could hardly get my words out. I shouted again,

"Get out, get out!"

Then I realized that all the men were looking straight at me. They didn't appear to understand English. Their faces were stern and as the lamps flickered in my eyes, I decided that they were ready to do something to hurt me. Mr. Alusion shouted,

"Butt madame", well it sounded like that! (It's actually Bhata meaning rice).

Then I heard Mostofa's voice,

"Rice ma'am."

Only then did I see that there was a table at the end of the room. The men went to sit on chairs and some women served them with bowls of rice. Mostofa spoke to me again.

"Rice ma'am, please, come eat."

I was being invited to eat some rice.

"No, no, no, please go away." I replied.

I was still traumatised in this awkward and scary situation and I wanted to run away and hide, but there was no-where to go.

I heard them talking as they ate their midnight feast. I wasn't going to join with them or eat anything when I didn't know what they were going to do to me. In my hysteria I wrapped myself in the mosquito net that was hanging over the side of the bed from the ceiling. All the time I was praying, Lord Jesus help me please. Make me invisible, don't let them see me. The oil lamps were on the table and the men's faces glimmered in the flickering light. Their demeanour had changed and they laughed and talked as they ate. I now know that these men were farmers and after working long hours outside they would eat at midnight in the cool of the night. However, at that moment my fears had taken a tight hold on me and I didn't move from my huddled position on the bed, wrapped in the mosquito net. I tried to control my breathing as I needed to get a grip on myself and I gradually calmed down as I heard the words of the Lord,

"I will never leave you or forsake you."(Heb.13 v. 5) and

"I will be with you unto the end of the world."(Matt.28 v20)

And that's where it seemed I was.

What felt like hours passed before they finished eating and drinking. I remained silent. I knew now that there were some women around, they had come in through a different door somewhere behind the table. Finally, as the men were leaving the room via the corridor, through tears of fear, I called to Mostofa,

"Please bring me a woman to sleep by me."

He conveyed the message to Mr. Alusion and within minutes I had a young girl beside me on the narrow bed and an elderly lady at my feet. My stomach was still churning with both hunger and trauma but at least the ordeal was over. I felt more at ease as the Lord once again had come to my rescue in this awful place. I dozed off again and woke to the sound of cocks crowing which signifies the crack of dawn in whatever country you are in.

Before the men came in to eat, I was yet again overcome by fear, my body had stiffened and sweat was coming from my brow, my heart was palpitating and sweat dripped down my back. I had asked Jesus to help me through the night and let me wake up early in the morning when the cock crows. Indeed, the Lord heard my prayers and it was morning at last. I noticed that the two ladies had left me and I was quite alone. There was a small square opening in the toilet area through which I could see the light of dawn. I didn't know what this day held for me but I was definitely NOT going any further. I would tell them to take me back to Narsingdi.

After a couple of hours I heard movement in the corridor and Mostofa came in and said we they were ready to leave. I washed my face with cream and a tissue. I was poised ready to tell Mr. Alusion that I didn't want to go any further and please take me back. I was so relieved to get out of that room and out of that house. In the daylight I could see the poverty they lived in. The women peeked out from another barn-like building, holding their scarves over their faces, as if afraid that I might see them. They were small in stature and looked emaciated, wearing dull coloured saris that didn't do them any justice at all.

My Father's house

I was about to ask Mostofa to tell Mr. Alusion to take me back when two men pulled up on motorbikes to speak with him. Mostofa told me that these men were my relatives and had heard about the English Begum Saab who had come looking for her father's people. They asked us to follow them and that it wasn't too far away. We headed east out of the village and onto a road surrounded by fields. We arrived at a place that was just like a villa with many outbuildings surrounding a piazza, a central place. Mostofa whispered to me, "This is what your father built, this is your father's house."

I looked on in utter amazement. Had I really found my father's people? By now many people had gathered in the courtyard, men, women and children, all looking at me but smiling. Old and young alike were inquisitive and interested to see me. It transpired that they were all my father's family. Whilst I stood in wonder, the men on the motorbikes introduced

themselves to me by name and smiled. Then one by one all the
menfolk gave me their names and I was told that they were my
blood relatives. Some of their faces had similar features to mine,
albeit they were men. None of the women came up to me to
introduce themselves, but this was their custom and etiquette
which I was aware of. They were not allowed to do that in front
of the men. They would do it later when they served me some
food.

Mostofa said that first I would be shown to my father's,
grandparent's, and Uncle Tariq's graves. We just walked outside
the compound into an area that was fenced off. It was actually
a small garden but it had become quite overgrown. It was now
the fiftieth year of my father's demise and I thought that was
significant. Most of the family stayed outside the garden, but I
followed the two motor cyclists who had brought us here. They
pointed out the exact spot where father's remains were laid.
There was no stone or wooden marker to say who was buried
there. Finally I was here, but with all the villagers watching I
wondered what should I do?

Beside Father's grave

I had to do something, but what? I decided that I would
pray, so after walking round the grave I started thanking Father

God for giving me my heart's desire in finding my father and his people. I lifted my hands to heaven and asked Father God to forgive the wicked uncles who had killed my father and who had taken over his estate and moved their families in; who had thrown my baby brother into the paddy fields to die, and left my mother a widow. She in turn left me and my siblings as orphans. I thought that prayer of forgiveness was important to me and to them. I am sure that none of this third generation of my father knew anything about what happened. I actually felt nothing to be honest. I wasn't sad or angry, I just felt awkward. I came out of the garden graveyard and followed the two men to one of my uncle's tombs where they in turn prayed to their god. Then I took some photos.

As I re-entered the courtyard a very tiny old lady came running towards me. I bent down to say hello and she cupped my face in her hands.

Tears ran down her face and she pinched my cheeks gently, and Mostofa translated as she spoke,
"Your face is as his face."
"Who?" I asked.
"Your brother Manikur, the boy with the grey eyes."

219

She went on to say that she was the woman who had rescued my brother from the paddy-fields. So the story Manikur told me was true.

Now I could meet the women. I was taken into one of the little houses and offered food. There were women here and they held their babies in their arms. It was quite dark inside and I could only see a bed, a table and a chair. I sat on the bed and listened as the women told me their names and how they were related to me. I was given rice, vegetables and fruit, then I had a tour of the villa. There were immaculately dressed young men with turbans on their heads. They looked like students and later on I was told that my grandfather and father had set up a faculty for teaching the Koran.

I was well satisfied now that my goal had been achieved and my eyes had seen for themselves, and that I had found out more than I had ever dreamed of. After many goodbyes and invitations to come again, we set off for the journey back to Narsingdi.

I had time to reflect. I thought about my father's brother Tariq who had been brought to London to work at the tender age of seventeen. He was only there a few months when he fell down some stone steps and died. My father took his body back to his village to be buried. Grandfather Lutfa's wife was buried in the same place. They only had two sons and one daughter, so he must have been very sad at these great losses, if he was still alive at the time.

The journey back was without event. We returned via the same route as we had come, fording the river with the pulley rope, it wasn't so daunting this time. The journey passed quickly and we were soon in Narsingdi. After thanking Mr.Alusion and the men, I was glad to see Popy's smiling face. As she prepared some food for me, I was able to relate to her all that had happened. So much easier as Popy speaks good English.

The Christian brothers and sisters of The Sacrifice Trust in Dhaka had been praying for me continuously and sending me texts, I was so grateful for their prayerful support and lifeline. As I look back it was a bit of a crazy venture. God had given me the free first-class ticket so I had to take the opportunity He had given me to pursue my life-long ambition to find my father's people. Mostofa, Momen, Popy, her daughter Mahek and her mother Jamina escorted me back to Dhaka on the bus and finally to the airport. With tears in their eyes they told me to come back soon. It was with mixed emotions that I boarded that plane. Settled in my first-class seat I was feeling very happy, satisfied and thankful that only God could do it this way. I slept all the way home!

To be fair, although my fears had gotten the better of me, Mr.Alusion and his men were looking after my safety and security. It was my own lack of faith, my own vain imaginations and my insecurities that had caused me to become so traumatised. In my soul I had been to hell and back. I can only give thanks for Mr.Alusion and his men for making a way for me to find my family and for looking after me as he saw fit BUT ultimately I was in God's hands.

Me with Mr Alusion and his family

221

Preaching in The Worship Centre in Blantyre.
The late Mrs Helen Singh as my translator

Alison with the ladies of Dedza mountain on a previous visit

Chapter 21

Malawi

I have developed a great love for Africa, having visited several different African countries but God had now laid Malawi on my heart. I had a lot of Malawian friends where I lived at the time. On one occasion the church in Bolton was having an African Sunday. The Pastors were from Malawi, so I knew it would be informative as they shared about their work with the poor children and orphans. This was where I met Peter Yates and his wife Margie. On speaking to them I found out that they lived in Cheshire, just four miles from where I now lived.

I have been to Malawi a few times with my dear friend, Mrs. Rosemary Agente, who was a prominent business women and owned a blanket factory. She had been a High Court judge and the first African woman to work for the American Embassy, based in Blantyre. She was the first woman driver in Malawi and was once a journalist who covered the Queen's visit there. She has written several books about her native people, "The Yaw," their traditions, culture and her memories of growing up in a small, poor village with her grandmother. She was the first African woman to own a castle. Sabini's castle is now called Blantyre and used for training the military.

Rosemary bought the land adjacent to the castle. It is a vast estate called Mapanga and we would always stay there in her beloved house. From there I was able to go to many towns and villages to preach and evangelise.

My main invitation was from Mrs. Singh, who was a lovely Christian lady. She was a candidate for the presidency for the second time running. Mrs. Singh had set up The Worship Centre in Blantyre, and every day at 12 noon over three hundred business people would forfeit their lunch to come to worship and pray. Everyday there was a different speaker. She asked me to speak and I very willingly agreed, then she told me later that I was to speak for five days in a row. I was taken aback but trusted the Lord to fill my mouth with His Word. And so it was.

At the end of the five days they gave me a love offering. Along with speeches of great honour, they presented me with a big bag of money, which in turn I gave back to the Pastor. I asked them if they would buy some bibles for me and deliver them to Mapanga. Over three hundred bibles were bought with that money and we were able to distribute them ourselves as we went from town to village, preaching and teaching. Oh what happy memories!

Peter and his daughter had been to Malawi with a view to helping the poor children and widows. He had met a young man called Moses, who lived at the bottom of Dedza Mountain. Moses heart was to take the Gospel of Jesus up the mountain to all the small villages where there were many AIDs orphans and women who were left to find a meagre living by toiling the very dry and arid land.

God put it on Peter and Margie's heart to adopt Moses and Grace, his wife, as their son and daughter. They all had the same vision to feed the orphans, to look after the widows and to preach the Gospel of Good News.

Back at home I began to meet with Peter and Margie and we prayed for the work in Malawi. As the years went by Moses became a very good Pastor, setting up little fellowships in the surrounding villages and with Peter sending out a small monthly allowance, Moses and Grace were now feeding the local poor children with porridge three times a week. The work has continued to grow and Pastor Moses is now a Bishop, overseeing more than seventy church groups all over the vast area of Dedza and beyond. Pastor Moses also trained one hundred and twenty local men to go out to unreached villages, travelling endless miles on bicycles, to share the love of Christ. He has set up three bible schools for the youth and his trainee pastors. Besides the micro finance projects and co-operatives, the ever-changing weather and illness affects the lives of the people from day to day. Droughts, flooding, AIDs and now Covid 19 kill people every day. It is a very challenging work but because of the love, trust, and faithfulness of two men, who live in the opposite sides of the world, this work has flourished. It's phenomenal and only God could have put us together to fulfil His vision in Malawi. All things are possible with God, even the impossible.

I have a great respect and love for both of these men of God, and their wives. As we have partnered over fourteen years in faith, love and obedience to the call of God on our lives, it has been a privilege to see the enormity of the work in building the church, helping the men, women and children of Dedza Mountain and how it has grown from a mustard seed to a harvest fit for The King. Only Jesus could have done such a thing as he worked in the hearts of men and women who are obedient to the call to Malawi.

Peter is a trustee of The Sunflower Trust and has passed the overseeing of this work to me. In 2020 Pastor Moses and his wife Grace had been invited over to England by the church and some friends for a holiday and to give him the opportunity to preach and share his work with others. I should have been heading over to Malawi to bring him. Unfortunately, due to circumstances beyond our control, he was not able to get a visa and the trip had to be cancelled.

However, God had another plan.

The Glory People

I had made the acquaintance of James Kotey from Ghana, when he was staying in the UK with The Glory People. Their ministry of praise and worship had brought them to the Oasis Christian Fellowship in Penmaenmawr, North Wales. The Glory People had been together for many, many years and although most of them range from sixty to eighty years old, they play instruments and sing their gospel songs and choruses like sixteen year olds. I always enjoy going to see them and to meet up with my Welsh Christian brothers and sisters in the Lord.

In 2018, when I was at The Oasis Christian Fellowship, I felt a prompting to go and speak to an African man who told me his name was James. I didn't know who he was or where he was from, but I had a word from God for him. It sounds like a cliché I know, but he was just there, right at the back, smiling, clapping and dancing away. God told me to say to him,

"Don't be in despair, because God is going to use your situation for His glory and your ministry will increase."

He was really taken aback, especially when I went on to tell him that he would suffer persecution and rivalry, but this was to spur him forward to fulfil his destiny in Christ. We swopped phone details and then I carried on enjoying the meeting.

I encountered him again over a year later at The Glory People's convention in Somerset. He called me a prophetess and said that all I had spoken had come to pass. God had promised him that he would become a bishop. Already he was church planting and doing evangelistic outreaches all over Ghana and Nigeria. He now had twenty eight churches. I was awestruck when he asked me if I would like to go to Ghana to do a crusade and some evangelistic missions around Accra and also visit some of the twenty eight churches situated in the more remote villages. Well, I thought about it and prayed!

Jason

I first met Jason a few years ago when I was in Manchester city centre with my niece. He was a street evangelist and was with another Christian man called Kieran. Kieran carried a large wooden cross as a prompt for people to ask him what he was doing and why? He would then take the opportunity to explain the Gospel message of Jesus Christ to them very effectively. The two men cordially invited me and my niece to one of their house fellowships just outside the city.

We decided to go as I esteem a personal invitation as something special. The fellowship was hosted by Naomi and her house was not too far away. It was a meeting for evangelists and there were about ten of us gathered in her dining room. We were invited to give our testimonies. The people were amazed and quite taken aback at the lives we had lived and suffered to get to this point where we were hard and fast evangelists, and I, an international minister and missionary.

It was a few months later when my sister Rose and I encountered Jason again in a totally different area at a praise and worship evening. He had gone up for prayer and looked troubled. I was able to corner him on his way back, prayed for him and gave him a prophetic word about a wife. Again I didn't see Jason for about six months. When I was next in the area I visited with Naomi and Jason happened to be there. He was delighted to tell me that God had heard our prayer for a wife, and that he was going to marry a lovely Christian woman in Ghana!

My eyebrows raised at first as I thought it wasn't a good idea but I kept my thoughts to myself. He had brought the woman, called Dorcas, over on one occasion, but I had missed seeing her. The photographs showed her to be very beautiful. She was the daughter of Bishop Cobbinah. I felt that this clarified that it was from God and an answer to prayer. A few months later Jason had gone to Ghana to marry her and start working as the Dean and head of the Bible Faculty in Accra, which belonged to his new father-in-law's church called The Lamb of God Ministries. It was a very prominent church with lots of sub-churches in the neighbouring villages. I kept thinking of Jason and Dorcas and promised that one day I would go to visit them.

Not on my agenda for 2020

A trip to Ghana was definitely not on my agenda for 2020. But that day came much sooner than expected. I had received an official invitation from Shofar Restoration Ministries belonging to Bishop James Kotey. I also had an invite to The Lamb of God Church and Bible Faculty from Pastor Jason and Dorcas Burns. His father-in-law, Bishop Cobbinah, had asked me to come to Accra. How could I refuse? As long as the dates covered two weekends, I could do the two crusades on one trip.

I already had a busy schedule. I had been to Tenerife in January, then spent a lovely time in Ireland and was planning a return trip in April, along with a visit to Hungary. In May I planned to go to Finland for the first two weeks. On my return I would prepare for Bishop Moses visit to the UK along with his wife. That would be for three weeks in June as requested by his sponsors, Peter and Margie, but I offered to host them. (As I said at the beginning, the visit was sadly cancelled in the end). However, I did have a vacant slot in March. Now I could take the opportunity to go to Ghana and contacted Bishop James Kotey and Pastor Jason to make the arrangements and the programmes for the crusades.

Next, I bought tickets to Accra for myself and ministry friend to fly out on March 5th. They were yet again affordable tickets enabling me to go in obedience to the call. My missionary friend would pay me for her ticket later. I have travelled on missions for over thirty years and as I have already said, I do not take any money from The Sunflower Trust to pay for flights. The Trust could not afford it and my policy is still the same, that anyone who comes with me must pay for their own flight and expenses or find a sponsor. This shows their commitment, passion and right motives from the heart.

As I write, the global pandemic of the dreadful Coronavirus was becoming quite concerning but I didn't realize just how bad it was. I had asked a few preachers and evangelists to pray about coming with me on this two week and two-part mission but because of the spread of the virus they politely declined, as did my co-missionary.

Finally, the day of my departure came, March 5th 2020. I had only arrived back from Ireland a few days before, having

228

spent time at Carrick Fergus by the sea near Belfast. It had been a time of preparation of prayer and prophecy for the trip to Ghana. Holy men of God had gathered at my friend Zoe's house and we had powerful unity in prayer. I was given the green light to go-ahead. I was so encouraged at a time when I felt totally inadequate to be the main speaker at two crusades and to lecture at the Bible Faculty, let alone preach at two Sunday services in two different churches with large congregations. I knew Africa and I knew they had high expectations of speakers and preachers. But,

"with God, all things are possible." (Matt.19 v 26)
When the Holy Spirit is with you, you can move mountains, take a nation and speak with His power. Doesn't it say in the bible?

"open your mouth and I will fill it." (Ps.81 v 10)
So now I knew that I had amazing spiritual back-up and prayer support behind me. The church I attend was in a pastoral transitional period, so knew nothing about my missions. I knew that I could rely on some of the congregation to pray for me. I hadn't really shared what I was going out to do in Jesus name. I go out on mission every month now, sometimes twice. I knew that this was my thirtieth missionary year and now in my late sixties, I wondered if things might change and if the ministry God had given me to do was at an end. However, missionaries never retire but they do re-fire! By God's good grace I hope a new challenge will come along.

The flight

I arrived at Manchester airport which all seemed quite normal and parked my car. Usually I would travel to the airport by train but, prompted by the Spirit, I went by car. The flight home was late night and an early morning arrival. Trains don't run that early. I was later to find out why taking the car was a wise thing to do.

Once in the airport I went to look at the departure board. I could see that a lot of flights had been cancelled or delayed.

People were starting to get concerned and irate. My flight was still up on the board. I was flying with KLM Dutch airlines which usually goes to Amsterdam first, then there would be a change to go on to your destination. This time my flight was going to Paris first, then a ninety minutes wait and then on to Accra, Ghana. As we were boarding, I realised that my flight to Paris was the only one not delayed or cancelled. All the disruption was caused by the virus pandemic and fleets of aircraft had now been grounded.

I arrived in Accra the next morning, after a very pleasant flight, with food on board and very attentive cabin crew. I slept most of the way even though it was often a good time to talk to people about my faith and life. Bishop James Kotey was meeting me and he took me to my accommodation at Bishop Cobbinah's church, which was situated on the other side of the city from him. The massive church and Bible Faculty in Kaisha district had a two bedroomed apartment which was up three flights of stone steps. Jason and Dorcas lived there.

The view was over their local community, which was a ghetto, and every day I could observe the daily activities of the locals, a life so different from mine. Bored looking men sat around smoking weed, lots of small children were playing barefoot in the rubble, and an old woman was foraging with a stick in the rubbish for plastic bottles to take to the recycler to earn some money. The younger women with babies on their backs were washing clothes in tubs or washing their small children who seemed to scream incessantly and very loudly.

Daily life in the township

The crusade

Bishop Kotey was picking me up about twelve noon and taking me to "The Love Feast," at his large newly built church called Shofar Revival Church. The feast was to celebrate the twenty-eight years that the church had been established. It just happened to coincide with his mother's birthday, and was also to welcome the prophetess's visit, did he mean me? Yes, he did, so I was the guest of honour and I sat at his table! I had to introduce myself and address the young pastors and youth.

231

Then I was introduced to the Bishop's wife, Pastor Theresa, who led us in worship and gave a short word. Next Bishop Kotey introduced me to everyone, I was very comfortable and happy in his presence. He had a real pastor's heart. He told me that he was one of seven children, he was the youngest and smallest. He began preaching at the age of eleven and has never stopped. He is a very powerful preacher and evangelist. I felt very privileged to be working for Jesus with him and his lovely wife.

I stood up, and shouted three times as I was led by the Spirit of God,

"Baruch haba B'shem Adoni"

(blessed is he who comes in the name of the Lord)

Out of my mouth came the sound of Yahweh and then the sound of the Shofar. I was amazed at how long my breath could hold the call, which is a call to repentance, preparation and danger. Now I was prepared and I knew I was far from alone, God was with me. At the gates of the church people were passing by and they stopped because they heard a strange sound of a woman whose voice sounded like a trumpet. Three of the people enquired of the church stewards what was going on and they were able to share the gospel with them. After the feast I was taken home to rest because at six o'clock I was to be driven to the crusade in the city. Well to me crusades are for the unsaved and basically for evangelism which I love. God has given me a loud voice and boldness to speak, so this was going to be an enjoyable way to serve the Lord. You know you have a gift and a calling when God uses you.

When we arrived the portable stage was already erected and the musicians were playing. We met up with Pastor Dorcas at my request. I wanted to give her opportunity to speak in the meeting. I was introduced to Pastor Mercy, she was to be my translator. She was a singer and roused the crowd that was forming. Bishop Kotey spoke briefly to open the meeting and then introduced me, again as a Prophetess from God and the U.K. This took their attention and the fact that I was the only light skinned face! The crowd then joined in the worship and the dancing.

Crusade in Accra

Just as the worship time was finishing a young man jumped up onto the podium and with Bishop Kotey's permission, took the microphone and sang with the most amazing voice. It stopped the passers-by who came closer, stood and listened. Then he gave the gospel message in their native language and led some of them through corporate prayer to the Lord.

Now it was my turn to speak and I prayed that God would fill my mouth with His word and in Jesus holy name He did just that. By the power of the Holy Spirit I gave the words out to the onlookers. I read from John Ch3, the account of Nicodemus who came to Jesus by night, enquiring about what it meant to be born again and how to reach the kingdom of heaven. Jesus replied,

"Verily, verily I say unto thee, except a man be born again, he cannot see The Kingdom of God." (John 3 v.3 KJV)

Jesus also said,

"Verily, verily I say unto thee, except a man be born of water
and of the Spirit, he cannot enter into The Kingdom of God.
That which is born of flesh is flesh and that which is born of the
Spirit is spirit." (John3 v 5 & 6)
I shouted the scripture out loudly. I had used it many times
before and knew it off by heart. I used the term Yahweh, Yeshua
and HaMashiach for Jesus. Then it happened!!! Just as I was in
full shout, the clouds burst their rain all over us and a mighty
wind came which nearly blew the platform and musical
instruments over. The team were frantically rushing round to
save everything from getting wet but I could not stop speaking,
even though the people were running for shelter or leaving. By
now it was very dark and I could not see the people but I carried
on shouting out my message, as did my very enthusiastic
translator, Pastor Mercy.

When it was over I felt a bit disappointed as I had not
had the opportunity to pray, anoint or to ask people if they
wanted to give their lives and souls to Jesus.

It was after midnight when I arrived back in my room,
very tired and deflated. This was to be a two day crusade,
continuing on the Sunday evening, and I felt worn out already.

Sunday service

The main Sunday morning service was usually attended
by more than one hundred and twenty people. On this day there
were more as it was Bishop Kotey's mother's birthday and they
had a visiting speaker (me). Some Ghanaians from America who
had come over to a relative's funeral, also attended the service.
So the church was packed.

This time I was led to speak from Luke 7, sharing the
account of the woman washing Jesus feet. After that I was
invited to pray over the people. I thought they meant
corporately but the people began to make a queue. I prayed and
was in the presence and power of God's Holy Spirit. I anointed
each person and prayed in the name of Yahweh, Yeshua and

HaMashiach. By the power of the Holy Spirit everyone was given a prophetic word and was prayed for. Over one hundred and thirty people were ministered to that day, they did not want to leave. My mouth was dry and my body exhausted but just when I thought it was the last dear soul, another would come. Oh, what a wonderful God we serve. There were many pastors in the congregation and they asked the Bishop if I could visit their churches, but I already had a full agenda.

Before I knew it, it was evening and we were returning to the city to finish the crusade. Miraculously there was no rain that night, but it was extremely hot! The stage was prepared, musicians and speakers in position and again I rose up and gave the gospel, this time demonstrating how Jesus was crucified. I got down on my knees and expounded how we must ask for forgiveness for our sins and how we have to ask Jesus into our hearts, as He is outside knocking.

"Behold, I stand at the door and knock, if any man hear my voice and open the door, I will sup with him and he with me.
(Rev.3 v 20)
I got up off my knees and rejoiced at Jesus hearing my prayer, and receiving me into His Kingdom, so that now I can enjoy a life with God the Father. At that I shouted,
"Come, come!!
"Come, unto me all you that labour and are heavy laden and I will give you rest." (Matt. 11v28)
At that the people came forward.

Always aware of my position I handed over to Bishop Kotey and he led them corporately to Christ. The Bishop told me that many people had said the prayer of repentance. His team had taken twenty-three names and phone numbers so that they could be contacted. It is not always for us to know how many, or who, but God knows.

I didn't was unaware that the singer who was in the crowd the night before, had already corporately led a multitude of people to Christ in his own native language which explained why I had thought no-one had responded to me on that first night.

Now, here on a warm Sunday night the people queued for me to pray for them and anoint them with oil. I gave the Bishop and his pastors some oil, and together we anointed and spoke prophetic words and prayers over them. It was after midnight again and we headed home, happy but exhausted. And that was only day two!!

Chapter 22

Out in the sticks!

On the Monday, Bishop Kotey picked Pastor Dorcas and I up to drive north to the coast for a few days of ministry. Pastor Dorcas accompanied us for the experience. We were going to visit a church plant on the way and it was arranged that we would to stay in the Bible College which was built by Shofar Ministries. From there we were going to teach and minister to the people in various rustic and very rural villages. The journey was tiring, it was very hot and the roads through the villages were just dirt tracks and pot holes. At one point, as we were driving up a mountain, I noticed a very big black cloud. The Bishop commented that it was exactly over where we were going. He had driven all the way and I had been enjoying the scenery of forests, the bush and the small villages with tiny shacks and mud huts. When it came, the thunder, lightning and rain were extreme and the dirt tracks became running streams and then small rivers.

The Bishop was driving a Cadillac which he had borrowed from a woman elder in his church. His four by four, which would have been more practical, was getting repaired. Eventually we arrived at the village where Bishop Kotey had bought the land, planted a church and placed a pastor to minister to the people. It was a delight to see and the villagers welcomed us warmly.

Regardless of the storm which had now abating, some of the people had turned out and were praising God. More people came as we were arriving. The word was given out and the people repented. They were full of expectation, hope and finally filled with the Holy Spirit as Jesus worked on their aching souls.

Each day we travelled to the outlying villages arriving in the afternoons and evenings to speak God's word. Some of the students from the Bible College accompanied us and shared in the teaching and ministry. Every day the Lord gave me a new word to expound to the people. The congregations numbered between fifty and seventy. We were welcomed everywhere we went and the word well-received. On the last day we were invited to the Police Academy. The students were welcoming, attentive and interacted with a joy and passion. We were served with a delicious lunch which was followed by a relaxing and sociable time on the beach. What a treat! All too soon we had to depart.

Now at this time, March 2020, the Coronavirus was spreading quickly but there were no cases in Ghana. We were advised not to be touching people or getting too close. In this area, the dear people needed a touch from Jesus and they got it. It's not that I am brave but my life experience is that I, Trust, Believe and Obey. I believe every word in the bible and rely on the Holy Spirit to direct me. Even if I get it wrong, I know that Jesus will rectify my mistakes and turn a bad situation into good.

In my thirty years of ministry my awesome Father God has been my guardian as I serve him round the globe. For now, the window of opportunity may be closing, but I took it and have had a wonderful life because of it. It has given me a life of abundance, joy, love, peace and hope. So, even my faith is a gift from Almighty God himself. Jesus sits at the right hand of God and intercedes for us day and night and it is He whom all these testimonies are about. We are servants, co-workers and kingdom builders, rewarded with hope, glory, and salvation. We have the nations for our inheritance.

My second week was spent with Bishop Cobbinah and the pastors and students of the Lamb of God church and Bible faculty in Accra. On the Friday I was taken a long way out to some villages where I was the speaker. The villagers gathered after a long, hot day working on the land. They had waited for our arrival for over an hour, but even in such a humble environment they had made a little podium and placed four chairs on it in honour of the Bishop, senior pastors and the

speaker. After much singing, worship and praise the Bishop gave an address, then he introduced me. Again I prayed,
"Dear Lord Jesus, fill my mouth with your words and not mine."

I esteemed this meeting, as poor as it was, it was just as important as one in any large church. Of course I had an outline prepared and a guideline of scriptures but I can't speak a word until I see the people's faces. The gathering was on the roadside, so there were little shops and stalls set up too. Even though it was after seven in the evening there was a lot of activity, hustle and bustle.

The Muslims are very busy in these villages. Like us, this is where they start trying to recruit local poor people into believing the Koran, but their false god does not love them or call them his children, he doesn't have the ability to forgive their sins or save their souls, they have to do it themselves by bowing down to Allah who has no son, no love and no peace. Our God loves us so much that He gave his son Jesus to die on a cross, to forgive and take away our sins once and for all. He shows his love everyday giving us life in abundance, grace and mercy, kindness and hope.

Now this is what I expounded very loudly to the people. I declared there is only one God, His name is Yahweh, and every other god is man-made. I shouted this over and over again and that Jesus is our Lord and Saviour. I told them that only those who believe on Him and give their heart, soul, body and mind to Him would be saved from hell and would have their place in heaven after they die. Very, very loudly I quoted from John 3 vs.3
"Verily, verily I say unto thee, except a man be born again, he cannot see The Kingdom of God."
and then from John 3 v.16,
"For God so loved the world that He gave His only begotten Son, that whosoever believeth in Him should not perish but have everlasting life."
Most of the people assembled were Christians already so I didn't make an altar call, but I anointed the Bishop and pastors and

gave them my oil from Jerusalem so that they could anoint their people. Although I didn't see or hear that anyone got saved, I am certain that God knows. I operate by the power of the Holy Spirit. I had proclaimed the gospel and I believed.

"So shall my word be that goeth forth out of my mouth: it shall not return unto me void, but shall accomplish that which I please, and it shall prosper in the thing whereto I sent it."
(Isaiah.55 vs.10-11).

The elders had never seen a white woman preach with such boldness and they were saying Amen and Hallelujah at every God given phrase.

It was very dark as we left and the people were still singing and dancing. It had been a wonderful and joyful meeting. I am invited to go back and stay as long as I want to. But I am only good for today and in these uncertain times, cannot promise anything. I do have a great love for the Ghanaian people.

Lamb of God crusade

Speaking at the Lamb of God Church

The next day was the crusade for the Lamb of God ministries and once again I was taken into the city to evangelise and preach the gospel. People went on their knees and repented asking God to forgive them. These crusades may not be in large arenas with sophisticated P.A. systems but the gospel of truth goes forth to a people whose hearts and ears have been prepared by God to respond.

"Faith comes by hearing and hearing the word of God."

(Rom.10 v 17)

I faithfully do my bit and God does the rest. I am just God's servant, the outcome is not my business. I do it for Jesus who saved me from myself, saved my soul and gave me a good reason to live, honour and serve. How could I do any less?

Sunday arrived and I was taken to the massive church building which could hold up to five hundred people. As in Anglican churches the bishop is highly honoured and his chair is like a throne. His wife sits on his left and the senior pastors on his right. I was seated there as well. I am used to working with the very poorest people in poor countries where etiquette is not needed, but this is Africa. Ghana was under British rule for decades and they taught this system of doing church. I am not against it because they have done a mighty work in keeping their nation a Christian one. Children are taught to honour their parents, to be hospitable and how to honour and entertain strangers. Families adopt and foster children with no help from the government. Education is a real priority and funded by Christian sponsors or the church. Many Ghanaians are lawyers, doctors, surgeons and business-people who are steeped in the Word of God which they take abroad with them to places like America and Europe.

Because my co-missionary had been unable to travel with me from the U.K. I was given her forty-five minutes speaking slot as well my own. Firstly, I gave my testimony which shocked the people at first but then delighted them as I told them about the thirty years of charity work and The Sunflower Trust ministry.

My message was to be about Obed-Edom. I received the message from a lovely Indian pastor in Wales one time. I had never heard the story before. It's found in the Old Testament in 2 Samuel and 1 and 2 Chronicles. For the next forty-five minutes I spoke on Obed Edom the Gittite from Gath, the town where the Goliath came from. In saying he would host the Ark of the Covenant, Obed Edom and his family were blessed. When David returned to move it to Jerusalem after three months, Obed chose to go as a bearer of the Ark, thus staying in relationship with God. He became a gate-keeper, a musician and a door keeper for the Ark. Eventually he became a worship leader and a priest. He stayed close to the Lord.

The story reminds us to stay with Jesus and look after the holiness in us. Be sanctified (set apart) for the holy work and be a worshipper. When we hold, carry, sing, follow, worship and praise the Holy One of Israel we also will be elevated to be a royal priesthood and a holy nation.

My voice shouted Yahweh and again the sound of the Shofar came out of my mouth, very loudly and for a long time. The people came forward for anointing, prayer and a prophetic word. They were not disappointed and right up to the last person they were ministered to, even the Bishop and his family. Oh, what a wonderful work had been done. The people lingered, thanking me and inviting me back.

During the service I had been presented with marvellous gifts of jewellery and a custom-made dress in the true, bright yellow colours of Ghana. I do not expect gifts, nor do I need them, but in thanking me and honouring me, they honour and receive the Lord who sent me. I am just a servant and a messenger.

Keep calm and PRAY

Because of the ministry, the meeting went on until about 4.p.m. It had started at 10.30 a.m! I was tired and having climbed the thirty-six steps up to the apartment I felt bodily exhausted, even though I was still buzzing in the Spirit. As I lay down on the bed, I felt prompted in my spirit to look at my flight details and start booking in for my flight home on the night of the 17th March. I would arrive home on the morning of the 18th. I got up and tried to log in. My phone wasn't working as I had no internet. I asked Pastor Jason what he thought about the situation and he said he would check on his internet. He could see that there didn't appear to be a flight listed and coronavirus was causing havoc to the aeroplane industry. There was talk that the Ghanaian president was shutting down his borders and closing the airport which in fact happened on the 21st March.

I realised that I needed to act quickly so although the next day was only Monday, I felt anxious and wanted to get a flight home as soon as possible. I relied on Pastor Jason and Dorcas for my communication, but here there was no electricity for periods of time and no reliable internet reception either.

I felt hot and mithered. There wasn't a pump to pump water up to the apartment for the toilet or kitchen, or to wash, it had to be brought up in buckets by Dorcas and her sister. But being a seasoned missionary, I was used to improvising and can manage in all situations. Praise the Lord.

We decided that we would go to the airport in Accra the next day so that I would be able to ask about my flight to the UK or due to the escalating gravity of the situation just be happy to get back to Europe, then somehow get to the coast and catch a ferry back to the UK. There I go again, sometimes my flesh over-rides my faith and I had momentarily forgotten that I know by experience that God will make a way.

I packed my belongings and we caught a taxi to the airport and then a shuttle bus to the other departure terminal, only to be met by security and told that I could not go in.

Everyone was masked and gloved. I was astounded! Now Lord, I need Your wisdom. I felt led to go to the KLM offices personally so I could speak with a representative. It was a short walk from the airport. There appeared to be fifty or so people queuing. God has given me patience, so I waited. Then I realised I needed to take a ticket and I discovered that I was number 133 in the queue!! Now I understood why so many people were waiting outside for their number to come up. A few missed their slot, some were shouting, others swearing and cursing the Ghanaian staff who were representatives for KLM. In situations like this you have to keep calm and PRAY.

After five long hours waiting in the cool of the waiting room my number came up. I stated my concerns about my flight on the 17th but I had already made the decision to buy the next flight out of Africa into the UK, or anywhere in Europe. I was calm and the rep was kind and understanding. I had prayed that I would get this rep because he was one of two men dealing with people's flights and they were from all over the world. The three lady reps were very stressed by the volume of people and trying to find them flights to get them home. At that time, with no corona virus outbreak in Ghana, the flights were a mandatory precaution to get people out and close up the country. The rep found me a flight at 11p.m. for that night (March 16th) to Manchester via Amsterdam, it would cost one hundred and fifty-seven dollars but I was so grateful. My ticket was issued. There was only one seat left!

Pastor Jason, Dorcas and I were very relieved. While we were waiting, I had asked Dorcas to use her mobile phone to find some cheap accommodation near the airport that would sleep three people, so that we could all rest. It was a wise thing to do because if I didn't get a flight at least we had a bed for the night and we could get a much needed shower and some food. I did have a flask of cold water and a packet of sandwiches at the ready if need be. I was planning to stay around the airport until I did get a flight home, once in the airport I was not coming out!

Dorcas had found a little lodge close to the airport and we went to get a shower and freshen up. Then took a short stroll to a nearby restaurant, where we enjoyed a good meal. I ordered a taxi for 9pm that evening to take me back to the airport.

The flight came in and I was pleased to be boarding especially as I knew I had the last available seat. I worshipped and praised God for looking after me once again. My Father is always there to help his daughter whose name is written on the palm of His hand. The return flight was pleasant, although I was squashed in a middle seat of four. I was happy. I didn't witness to anyone as it was night-time for most of the flight and everyone slept, including me.

I was very shocked when I arrived in Schiphol airport Amsterdam, it was devoid of planes and people. Those I did see were dressed in white all in one suits, masks and gloves. It was very scary but at least I was in Europe. If the worst came to the worst I could stay with my 'adopted' son Wynand who worked in Amsterdam but lives in Rotterdam. Yet again my earthly logical thinking, as ever trying to work out the "what ifs." Thank God that His ways are higher than our ways.

The flight was called and when I arrived back in Manchester it was eerie. There was a lack of people, the planes were grounded and all parked in rows. I hurried myself through passport control and then waited outside the airport for an airport bus to take me to the carpark. The atmosphere alone at the airport, although it was empty, was heavy with an evilness in the air.

Oh, what a momentous feeling I had as I started up my car and was homeward bound. Now I knew why I had used my car to take me to the airport. I was elated to be home to my family who were all willing to fill me in with the latest events even before I had the opportunity to share my news.

Epilogue

As I have written this book, I have realised all the more that God has wrought many miracles in my life and in the lives of many others. I have tried to convey to the reader how my life of insignificance, sorrows and pain was, and still is, used for God's glory. He trained me from a young age to suffer and endure, as I was parentless, homeless, and quite unloved. I rebelled against authority and was ever looking for love.

Everything I needed was all found in Jesus. At the age of thirty- eight God revealed His love and parenthood to me. It was He who completely changed my life. He gave me worthiness. It was He who lifted me up and guided me in the direction and path He would take me on. Knowing that God Himself thought that I was valuable enough to be bought back by His death on the cross. On my part I was so grateful to be found by God. He taught me, by His Holy Spirit, to be a teacher, preacher, evangelist, missionary and historian. I could do nothing by myself. I had to learn to be teachable and as God renewed my mind and ways of thinking, everything I did was for Him, through Him and in Him.

"Be not conformed to this world but be you transformed by the renewing of your mind that you may prove what is that good and acceptable and perfect will of God, then you will learn to know God's will which is good, pleasing and perfect.

(Rom.12 v 2)

The old me had to go. A new person emerged, one that was pliable and willing to just serve this mighty God, to understand His purposes and His will, so I could do what He wanted me to do.

"Therefore, if any man be in Christ he is a new creature, old things are passed away, behold, all things are become new."

(2 Cor.5 v 17)

This book is a witness to my God and my Lord and Saviour who saved me from myself and satan. Jesus, my God who died on the cross so that my sin is forgiven, gave me a powerful testimony and life of abundance. Happiness and joy became my new norm. I haven't got words to say how grateful and thankful I am that He saved my soul and gave me a new life with the risen Christ. This book can only reflect a little of all the things that God, the Great Jehovah, did for me and my family and my experiences and adventures of which there have been so many. I've counted over fifty countries where the Lord Jesus has taken me to and there He has filled me with the Holy Spirit and anointed me to

"preach the Gospel to the poor." (Luke 4 v.18)

He enabled and empowered me to look after widows and orphans, to pray for the sick and to intercede for others. By His grace He taught me to speak in other tongues and understand people's ways and languages. I've loved every precious moment of serving my King Jesus, my Lord of Lords. I urge you who have read this book, to read The Bible and hand your life over to Christ and give Him your requests. He will change you and strengthen you beyond your wildest dreams.

Remember I said, missionaries do not retire but refire and maybe God would bring me a new challenge. Well, you will never guess what happened next...

Printed in Great Britain
by Amazon